FINANCE FOR THE NEWLY ADULTED

A FINANCIAL DICTIONARY FOR EVERY HOUSEHOLD

GUY EDWARDS

© **Copyright 2023 - Guy Edwards. All rights reserved.**

It is not legal to reproduce, duplicate, or transmit any part of this document in either electronic means or in printed format. Recording of this publication is strictly prohibited and any storage of this document is not allowed unless with written permission from the publisher except for the use of brief quotations in a book review.

Disclaimer Notice:

Please note the information contained within this book is for educational and entertainment purposes only. All effort has been executed to present accurate, up-to-date, reliable, and complete information, but no warranties of any kind are declared or implied. The content within this book has been derived from various sources that were verifiable at the time.

By reading this notice, the reader agrees that under no circumstances is the author responsible for any losses, direct or indirect, that are incurred because of the use of the information contained within this book, including, but not limited to, errors, omissions, or inaccuracies.

CONTENTS

Introduction — 7

1. KEY CONCEPTS OF PERSONAL FINANCE — 13
   Money Management — 14
   Financial Literacy — 19
   What Are the Necessary Steps for Successful Money Management? — 26

2. GETTING STARTED WITH BANKING — 33
   Why Do You Need a Bank Account? — 35
   Different Types of Bank Accounts — 39
   Understanding Interest Rates on Your Bank Accounts — 45
   How to Select a Bank that Suits Your Needs — 46
   Choose a Specific Organization — 49

3. SETTING FINANCIAL GOALS — 55
   The Importance of Financial Goals — 56
   How to Set Efficient Financial Goals with the SMART Formula — 60
   What to Consider when Deciding on Your Financial Goals — 65
   Adjusting Financial Goals — 68

4. BUDGETING AND SAVING — 73
   What is a Budget? — 74
   Common Budgeting Pitfalls — 79
   Building Your Budget — 82
   What Proportion of Your Salary Should You Save? — 85
   Building an Emergency Fund — 86

5. MANAGING CREDIT 89
   What is Credit? 90
   Credit Scores, Reports, and Freezes 92
   Building and Improving Your Credit
   Score 97
   What You Should Know About Credit
   Cards 100

6. UNDERSTANDING LOANS, LENDERS,
   AND BORROWERS 107
   What is a Loan? 108
   Reasons Why You May Want a Loan at
   Some Point 109
   Different Types of Loans 112
   Interest and Principal 115
   Interest Rates Explained 116
   Lenders and Borrowers 121
   How to Compare Loan Conditions 124

7. AVOIDING AND ELIMINATING DEBT 127
   What is Debt? 128
   Different Types of Debt 130
   How to Prevent Yourself from Building
   Up Bad Debt 132
   How to Eliminate Debt 134

8. PREPARING FOR LATER: WORKPLACE
   RETIREMENT PLANS 139
   Employer-Sponsored Retirement Plans ... 140
   Varieties of Non-Employer-Sponsored
   Retirement Programs 156

9. INVESTMENT BASICS 167
   What is Investing? 168
   Pros and Cons of Investing 169
   Investment Principles 171
   Different Types of Investments 172
   How to Assess Your Investment
   Readiness 175

Investment Strategies for Beginners 176
Mistakes to Avoid When You Start
Investing 178
Pitfalls of Following Trendy Investments 180
Investing with Mutual Funds 184
Should You Use a Financial Advisor? 188
Using Your Investments to Get You Even
More Money 191

Conclusion 195
References 199

INTRODUCTION

"Financial freedom is available to those who learn about it and work for it." —Robert Kiyosaki.

My good friend Richard cleared ten years' credit in thirteen months because he deftly implemented discipline. His debt cycle started after he applied for a *Discover* card in college to receive a free cooler. He had six credit cards with balances totaling $18,000 and interest charges between 12 and 14 percent.

One day, as we talked about his rising debt profile, he began to consider the cash he had thrown away on finance payments. He resolved to pay off his debt within a year, so he constructed an Excel spreadsheet and entered his monthly payments, credit-card balances, and interest rates. He then started paying the most significant amount he could on credit with the greatest interest.

Richard didn't make much money working for a nonprofit foundation, so nearly 50% of his earnings paid off his debt. After automating his payment to avoid changing his mind, he noticed that he was shelling out several hundred dollars each month on eating out, streaming services, and app subscriptions after reviewing his receipts. Richard carried a copy of the spreadsheet in his wallet, which made him consult it when purchasing. He was debt-free after a little more than a year.

If you're reading this, you don't know how to incorporate healthy financial habits. This may be because of your parents or caretakers needing better financial habits or just trusting that school will teach you to manage money.

Several years ago, I had this challenge and was scared of the future and what would happen if I didn't become financially literate. My fear was increased by bad news about the state of the economy, climate change, and other concerning factors I heard in the report.

I didn't want to work myself into burnout because I wanted to enjoy life. I concluded that I had to look for ways to work smarter, not harder, with my money, scared of being unable to achieve or maintain a similar quality of life as my parents.

I dreamed of a luxurious lifestyle that I couldn't afford, and that my family could never afford, so I started looking for ways to live the lifestyle I see celebrities, influencers, and maybe even wealthy friends display on social media.

If you want to be debt-free, create generational wealth, or attain financial freedom, mastering money management and budgeting can help. Being financially illiterate or lacking in financial management from birth or up is nothing to be embarrassed about. Educating yourself is the most critical step toward financial freedom. I understand your current financial situation—having experienced it myself—and will show you practical strategies to improve your finances.

What will you benefit from this book—you will:

- Walk through all critical aspects of financial literacy and discover creative strategies to succeed with your wealth-building efforts.

- Learn how to define realistic yet challenging goals, achieve them, avoid financial mistakes and going into debt, and prepare for retirement.
- Understand bank interest rates and how to create the account type that supports your short or long-term financial objectives.
- Eliminate the unhealthy choices, making you splurge, boost your savings capacity, bypass the common pitfalls threatening your budget, and build your credit rating.
- Discover basic loan types, including their characteristics, learn practical procedures for comparing loan conditions when requiring credits, and understand effortless debt repayment strategies.
- Identify viable investment vehicles and strategies to create wealth, learn from previous investors' mistakes, and acquire the successful tips investing requires.

My background in Finance and business administration, combined with my personal experience, gives you a well-rounded perspective on the path to financial success. I know what it takes to create wealth and stable finances in today's economy.

With this book, I plan to prepare young adults and professionals for a successful financial future. This should be a go-to book for you to keep for years and pick up whenever you want to research any fundamental financial topic.

Suppose you have problems incorporating healthy financial habits, want debt-free, or want to build a solid financial future. In that case, you will find the necessary support in this book.

Join me, Guy Edward, as I set you up for the financial future of your dreams. Start into adulthood with the knowledge you need to build wealth and master your finances right from the start, and use it to guide you as you go through each financial milestone. Your journey to a secured future starts with *Key Concepts of Personal Finance*, Chapter One's focus.

KEY CONCEPTS OF PERSONAL FINANCE

Whether you are saving for a vehicle or your pension, handling your finances is essential for leading a self-reliant and safe life. Personal finance is assessing your economic state, including your revenue and objectives, and routinely allocating funds to required costs (Bitpanda, n.d.). It takes a lifetime to develop the habit of managing your money.

Since your requirements and circumstances about money may alter as you advance, review your financial objectives and make necessary adjustments.

Personal finance describes many aspects that are important for the monetary success of individuals— understanding its key concepts before getting started so

MONEY MANAGEMENT

that you are aware of the "why" behind every critical step towards financial freedom.

Money management describes the monitoring and planning of a person's or an organization's use of capital. Money management frequently comprises earning, investing, and trading. It also provides investment management and portfolio management (CFI, 2023).

Using *money management* and *budgeting* in the context of personal finance is quite common. Financial planning can help with proactive money management. Individuals have various financial plans due to several considerations, including lifestyles, varying ages, and family structures.

The core ideas behind budgeting can be applied universally. For instance, the *50-30-20* rule is a simple personal budgeting strategy. Based on these guidelines, people can allocate 50% of their post-tax income to necessities (such as food, mortgages, and utilities), spend 30% on wants (like taking trips or seeing movies), and save or invest the remaining 20% (CFI, 2023).

Reduce unnecessary spending by using budgeting and planning techniques. Good money management helps people reduce the risks of having insufficient funds, encouraging them to achieve their long-term objectives.

Learning Cash Management

Investors frequently hire financial consultants for expert money management when their net worth rises. Financial advisors support comprehensive money management plans that include retirement and estate planning. They are typically connected to private banking and brokerage services (Chen, 2022).

Money management for investment companies is another essential component of the investment sector. Individual investors can choose from a wide range of investment funds that cover all classes of investable assets available in the financial market.

Money managers at investment companies assist their clients by providing investment solutions, endowments, and retirement plans.

Money Management Process

Create realistic objectives. Wanting to be a millionaire is an abstract financial goal because it does not specify the figure you aim for (or want to achieve). Having $2 million and retiring when you are 60 is a realistic goal (Money Lover, n.d.).

Building practical financial objectives requires planning. For example, you might need to:

- Establish a financial strategy with sufficient time and consideration.
- Create a path illustration and strive to follow it.

Suppose you want to spend $1,000 on iPhone X within the next 12 months. To achieve this objective, you must save roughly $84 each month.

Acquire the relevant tools. Establish a location where you feel free and safe to view any paper records on your finances. Everyone wants to keep their financial information private, so ensure it is secure.

Keep your paper records safe yet accessible to find what you need quickly.

Since most transactions are now completely paperless, you can save time and effort using software or money management applications. Some are available on the Play Store and the Apple Store.

Track payments. Always keep in mind that expenses must be less than revenue. Overspending and having credit card debt are the root causes of almost all financial issues (Money Lover, n.d.). Make payment tracking a fun exercise by following these practical steps:

- Monitor your earnings and expenses daily.
- Keep receipts. Retain them to remember your transactions at the day's end and recall what you paid for. You can also use a banking app on your phone to track payments.
- Generate monthly reports and review the findings once you have amassed sufficient data on everyday transactions.
- Examine each transaction individually to determine how your money was used.

Create a budget. Budgeting means setting aside a certain amount for housing, food, and education. Creating a budget can help you limit spending and increase savings.

Indicate your net income—this sum includes your net monthly payments from your employer and the average of all bonuses and other compensation you have received.

Provide a breakdown of your monthly spending. By tracking your payments, you can make an educated guess at your monthly totals and the sums for each category based on the daily and monthly data you have.

Make your budget—start with a spending plan for your essential needs, such as housing, food, transportation, and personal expenses. Want some ideas on how to make a budget? Using this guide may help:

- Set aside 10 percent or more of your income as a life emergency fund.
- Split the remaining funds between amusement and education.
- Decide where to make periodic financial changes after implementing a budget strategy.
- At least once per month, review and assess your budget.

Save money. You need an emergency fund to survive. It's not a good idea to put the funds in a bank account where you can be tempted to spend it for anything other than emergencies. Open a savings account where you can earn more interest over time by saving more.

Cash Management Advice

The ability to estimate and manage your income and schedule wages and debt payments is an essential skill for success. Managing cash involves taking these intelligent steps:

- When your pay increases, save the extra money rather than squander it.

- After paying off your debt, start putting money toward savings the next month.
- Save money despite your debt. Set cash aside for emergencies even though your savings are modest.
- Review your monthly budget and expenses every two weeks to remove any excessive spending.

FINANCIAL LITERACY

Financial literacy means comprehending and using various financial competencies successfully, such as managing finance, investing, and budgeting. Financially literate individuals become self-sufficient, allowing them to achieve financial independence. You can attain financial literacy by:

- Creating a budget, cutting costs, and protecting your funds. You can make wise purchases and invest money in worthwhile things.
- Understanding the distinction between good and bad debt. You constantly consider your entire portfolio, which includes your wages, savings, and investments.
- Recognizing your ignorance and seeking assistance when required. Not letting money

(or a lack of it) deprive you of success makes you financially literate (Ritchie, 2023).

Finance Fundamentals and Financial Education

Keep a record of your monthly spending. Write down each purchase you make in a journal or a mobile app. Be vigilant in this area because you can easily forget your payments.

Determine your fixed and variable costs. Fixed expenses include rent, mortgage, auto, electric, water, and student loan payments. Variable costs include food, pet supplies, grooming services, and concert tickets.

Total everything up. Determine your average monthly spending three months after you start. Check out the categories as well.

Examine your variable costs. Determine what aspect of these monthly payments brings you the most joy so that you can decide whether they are justified. Which of them can you live without?

Include savings. Set aside a portion for savings every pay period.

Make your budget now. Start implementing the necessary reductions in both your variable and fixed costs.

Establish your weekly or biweekly savings goals. Your required living expenses are the remaining funds.

A Detailed Summary of Savings, Debt, and Credit

Saving

Using a savings account, you can stop unforeseen expenses from depleting your monthly budget and gradually accumulate cash reserves for sizable future purchases.

Personal savings decreased 15% from $73,100 in 2021 to $62,086 in 2022. The least likely age group to have emergency funds is those between 30 to 49.

Sixty percent of Americans need more savings to pay for an unforeseen $500 or $1,000 bill. One out of every five adults close to retirement age has no savings (Ritchie, 2023).

Have a budget you can stick to, even if that means beginning small with $50 from each paycheck or canceling your gym membership to save $100 monthly.

Debt

During the past 40 years, personal debt has been rising slowly but steadily in America. American households carried an $890 billion credit card deficit, $1.59 trillion in student loans, and $11.39 trillion in mortgage debts (Ritchie, 2023).

Credit

Credit bureaus base scores on variables that represent your spending patterns. You establish your credit history when using plastic to make purchases.

The history of how frequently you borrow, how soon you repay it, and the amount you owe can shape your credit. Increasing your credit score can help you qualify for auto loans, mortgages, credit cards, and low-interest loans.

How Many People Understand Money Management?

Although there are only so many accurate ways to gauge how many individuals are financially educated, there need to be more specific competencies to support that assumption.

Approximately 20% of people would meet the criteria if you used the percentage of people who do not live from paycheck to paycheck. Budgeting also helps gauge financial literacy. How do we Americans fare in this regard? Regrettably, just one-third of those who receive a salary follow their budget (Ramsey Solutions, 2023).

Do You Have a Grasp of Your Finances?

Your response to these questions will determine whether you should classify yourself as financially knowledgeable.

Can you make a monthly plan that accounts for your essential costs, bills, debts, and sinking cash for upcoming purchases?

Do you currently have any debt? Or are you making a conscious effort to bring down your debt?

Do you know how much money you need to live on for three to six months?

Do you have access to an emergency fund that would enable you to avoid taking out loans in the case of a sudden, significant life crisis, like being laid off?

Do you understand how compound interest investments increase in value over time?

Do you understand the different types of insurance required to safeguard your funds and investments?

What Makes Financial Knowledge Crucial?

Differentiate needs from wants. Adults know the distinction between necessities and wants. Nevertheless, it might be simple for teenagers and tweens to mistake a want for a necessity.

Educating children about money may teach them to balance their wants and needs without incurring debt. Older kids may want to go on a vacation with their pals. However, with even a basic understanding of finance, they will realize they might need to budget and save money for this. (Paris, 2023).

Understand money's worth. Financial literacy paves the way for wise financial decisions today, resulting in better choices with more rewards.

Learn to put money to work. Discussions on advanced financial literacy could center on various investment options (such as higher-risk stocks or lower-risk investments) for growing wealth.

Attain financial freedom. Giving children the freedom to purchase their own designer clothing or pricey running sneakers will give them more confidence in managing their money as they age.

Kids can develop financial skills by choosing what to buy and the amount to spend on it on their own, with their parent's guidance.

Discover ways to bypass debt. If you are a parent, does the idea of your kid using a credit card in their name to shop at the mall or online make you nervous? Discussing credit is essential for ensuring that children comprehend the value of money and the repercussions of poor monetary decisions.

If your kid asks for a credit card, instead of immediately saying "no," try explaining that it's not free money. Use an online calculator to demonstrate how quickly credit card debt can accumulate if your arguments don't persuade your kid.

Uncover scams. We frequently use the internet, which makes us prey to hackers who dubiously strive to access our money.

You may avoid online scams by emphasizing the value of keeping your account details and password secure. Avoid clicking any weird or questionable links, even if they appear from a friend.

Real-world financial education also includes developing a knowledgeable consumer mindset. Inquire about a company's return policy before making a purchase. Conduct preliminary research before purchasing, such as comparing costs and reading internet reviews (Paris, 2023).

WHAT ARE THE NECESSARY STEPS FOR SUCCESSFUL MONEY MANAGEMENT?

Better money management can pay off if you put in the time. Keep track of your expenses and save a ton of money. Use your savings to settle debts, put money toward retirement, or go on a trip.

Make a roadmap. Make future purchases, significant investments, and ongoing spending a priority. With a road map to lead you, you will get far on your financial freedom journey (Opperman, n.d.). Engaging in fundamental money management requires planning.

Create financial objectives. List your financial goals. Every month, keep fostering and revising your plans. If you take stock of your weaknesses and acknowledge your successes, you're more likely to succeed if you put your goals in writing, so do it.

Prioritize saving. Put money aside for recurring needs like home and vehicle upkeep. If you save between five and ten percent of your earnings, you can build up the cash that lasts you for six months. Make saving a habit that you never break.

Study your financial condition. Decide on your monthly debt payments, recurring bills, and living costs. Compare monthly net revenue against expenses.

Know how much debt you owe overall and maintain a record of your earnings, expenses, and debts. Just like saving, make this a habit.

Maintain a reasonable budget. Learn to set a budget and stick to it as strictly as possible. Review your spending plan. Compare budgeted and actual spending.

Note your expenses. How do you assess your spending plan? Even after you begin following your new spending plan, keep tracking.

Knowing where your funds go is essential. Keeping a spending diary can help you determine where to make adjustments.

Separate needs from wants. Prioritize attending to your needs. Only when requirements have been fulfilled should money be spent on desires.

If you have a problem setting boundaries, consider answering this question before making purchases:

How did I survive without this for so long?

You can distinguish between necessities and wants using this response.

Keep expenses below income. Limit your monthly charges to what you pay to your creditors. If you discover your monthly expenses exceed your income, get help from a nonprofit credit counselor.

Be prudent when using credit. Use credit for pre-planned purchases, convenience, and safety. Calculate the maximum amount you can comfortably spend on credit and still be able to pay it off each month.

Limit your credit card spending to 20 percent of your net income. Avoid taking out loans to pay your creditors (Opperman, n.d.).

Pay bills quickly. Keep your credit score high. Contact your creditors and clarify the issue if you can't pay your debts on time.

Should I embrace private or joint money management?

You should exercise caution while managing joint finances if your partner has a poor credit rating. Your credit score can be affected whenever you create a joint bank account or buy a mortgage together (Money Helper, n.d.).

Before merging your finances, check your credit ratings.

Budgeting for an Irregular Paycheck or Earnings

You may have a variable or erratic monthly income if you have a zero-hours contract or are self-employed.

Even though you may not know your monthly income, you should know your monthly expenses. If you know your expenses, you can budget—this is an excellent method to find areas where you may also make savings.

Using Piggy Banks, Glass Jars, or Other Money-Management Tools

Keeping your funds organized and secure can be enjoyable using a piggy bank. Although buying a piggy bank or a glass jar is simple, nothing prevents you from crafting one if you could:

- Clearly understand your monthly or weekly income and outgoing expenses for this approach to be practical
- Decide on the type of budgeting container you want to employ
- Use containers like jam jars or envelopes, or create different bank accounts for each spending category as an alternative

When you use actual containers to create a budget, you take money out of the designated jar as bills come in to pay them. Before you go shopping, you follow a similar procedure.

Taking Care of a Missing Person's Finances

You might need to handle their financial affairs if a member of the family or close friend is missing.

Practical advice is available in this regard from the independent organization for missing persons (Money Helper, n.d.). The nonprofit organization can assist with whether:

- You and your missing relatives share assets.
- You rely on them for financial support.

The organization outlines when and how to handle a missing relative's finances and administer their estate when the circumstances show they are most likely dead.

Poor mental health and financial difficulties

It might be challenging to handle money when you are depressed, agitated, or anxious.

If you spend cash you don't have on items you don't need to make yourself feel good, you will only regret it later. When you converse on the phone, visit the bank, or open your bills, you might experience anxiety or stress.

Your impulsive behavior (such as spending a great deal of cash all at once) may result in the signs of a mental illness. If your income drops due to, say, having to stop working or taking time off due to illness, any of these issues could worsen.

Money management describes the monitoring and planning of a person's or an organization's use of capital.

Good money management helps people reduce the risks of having insufficient funds, encouraging them to achieve their long-term objectives.

Money managers at investment companies assist their clients by providing investment solutions, endowments, and retirement plans.

The critical aspect of building a secure financial life is learning to manage your money. Whether you want to purchase a car or make a down payment, minimizing expenses and improving your savings can help. You will learn banking basics in the upcoming chapter.

2

GETTING STARTED WITH BANKING

Banks handle various tasks, including money transfers, exchange rate trading, and asset management. They also offer credit facilities to borrowers using clients' funds. It's critical to comprehend key fundamentals before opening an account to make the most of banking services and avoid making expensive mistakes.

Knowing where to open an account and the variety of services banks provide are all part of it. Learn the charges and interest rates applicable to each account type.

Digital shift. Increased focus on client relationships. Future trends have many possible applications in the banking sector. (Money Gate, 2023). Many instances include:

Machine learning and artificial intelligence (AI)—these innovations may enhance financial assessment, customer relations, and identity verification.

Blockchain is a network that stores records in a manner that makes systemic changes, hacking, and cheating challenging or even impossible. It is simply a web of computer networks that duplicates and distributes a transaction log in digital form across the overall infrastructure. Using these advancements, you can track cash transactions safely and accurately, eliminating intermediary requirements.

Biometrics. Financial institutions may use biometric authentication, such as a thumbprint or face detection, to improve security and eliminate the password requirement.

Mobile payments. More people are expected to use their mobile phones to conduct financial activities like purchases or transfers.

Virtual and augmented reality. While *Augmented Reality* improves the realities by layering computer-generated data over it, *Virtual Reality* is the technology that generates adventures that feel nearly real and/or credible in a fabricated or digital fashion. The banking sector might use these systems for advertising, customer support, and research.

IoT (internet of things). Gadgets such as sensors can facilitate new methods of controlling and managing capital assets in the banking industry.

While most people get their first checking account in their teenage years, there are many more things to know about the finance system and how to utilize the advice from financial advisors, different bank accounts, and other aspects to advance financially.

WHY DO YOU NEED A BANK ACCOUNT?

Everyone can open a bank account; they are for more than just people with much money to stash away. To open an account, you need a passport, driver's license, or other state-issued identification cards.

Some financial institutions will open an account with other types of identification, like a foreign voter registration card. There are many good reasons to start utilizing a bank account to assist you in managing your money if you don't already.

Flexibility. You can pay your bills promptly online or with a check. Also, you will have bank statements as proof that you settled your accounts, which is less expensive than purchasing a money order (Latimer, n.d.).

You may withdraw money from an ATM or make purchases at stores if you get a debit card for the account. Most places that take credit cards also accept debit cards for payment.

Security. Although it may be tempting, you are not safe if you hide your funds under your mattress in case of a fire or burglary.

Your bank account is protected, which means that if your bank is looted, you won't lose any money.

Simple saving approach. Many banks will pay you interest when you deposit money into a savings account. Your money will gradually increase thanks to the interest. To avoid paying more in charges than you earn in interest, compare banks and understand all expenses (Latimer, n.d.).

Affordability. Credit unions and banks frequently provide their customers with free or inexpensive services.

Access to credit facilities. Banks frequently reward loyal customers, especially those who handle their finances carefully.

Quick cash lenders for modest loans can be expensive because of their high-interest rates and lending costs.

A Checking Account—Do I Need One?

Yes, that's the clear-cut and unequivocal response.

Your checking account can serve as a central location for all your financial transactions, assisting you in keeping track of your payments and adhering to your spending plan (FNBO, 2021).

Earn easily and quickly. Employers usually favor direct deposit for payments. Having a bank account and establishing direct deposit allows you to request that your employer transfer your paycheck into your checking account regularly.

Easy and quicker bill payment. While using online bill payment services, you can send checks and make simple card payments by connecting a debit card to your account.

Other people may also pay you via wire transfer or online payment.

Three Crucial Factors to Consider Before Opening a Checking Account

- **Can I pay the fees for my checking account?**

Banks frequently charge checking account service fees. They start with a monthly service fee for as long as your account is active. Many of these fees can be removed from your account by following simple guidelines set by the bank, be sure to ask about them.

Although these costs vary greatly, you may be charged $10 or more monthly, depending on your balances and banking habits. Over a year, this monthly cost may easily reach $120 or more (FNBO, 2021).

When comparing checking accounts, another cost to take into account is ATM fees. Some banks will charge when you utilize an ATM from one bank; however, the fee increases when you use another bank.

- **What should I do with my checking account?**

Security is crucial if you use your debit card for most purchases, especially if you shop online.

Paying bills like mortgage, cable, insurance, and utilities would be simple using mobile banking apps. Bill-paying checking accounts make it simple to expedite this procedure.

- **Should I maintain multiple checking accounts?**

Your bank account usage and money management will determine. Some maintain separate checking accounts to manage expenditures and pay bills. For simplicity of budgeting, it is recommended to use only one checking account for a household.

DIFFERENT TYPES OF BANK ACCOUNTS

Bank accounts have peculiar differences—while some have a minimum balance or fee requirements, others don't. Improper money withdrawal may trigger penalties for some people. Savings and checking accounts are excellent places for everyone to start (Ramsey Solutions, 2022).

Checking Account

You can obtain a checking account's debit card online or from a physical bank. Since it functions like cash, you no longer need to take out or carry as much cash.

You may shop for your goods at the supermarket or gas station with your debit card. The money is typically immediately taken out of your checking account. Spending within a budget and paying bills are also made simple with a checking account due to the visibility of transactions and immediate loss of checking account balance.

Your checking account is debited on the due date when you form an automatic bill payment. There's no need to scramble to get a stamp and an envelope to mail your mortgage payment or to forget to pay the electric bill (Ramsey Solutions, 2022).

Using a budgeting tool, you can link your bank account to your monthly budget, making it simple to keep track of all your spending and progress toward your financial objectives.

Savings Account

It's an excellent place to store money you don't immediately need but want to keep close by, just in case. You may have multiple savings accounts—for example, you could have different accounts for emergency, vacation, and house down payment savings. These will all have different balances but can be looked at in an app to keep tabs on your budget.

Keeping your funds in a savings account won't make you wealthy. Most average interest rates are less than one percent (Ramsey Solutions, 2022). However, it improves your ability to budget, strengthens your capacity to save, and provides you with a place to put the extra money you don't immediately need.

High-yield savings accounts (such as *Popular Direct*, *Bask Bank*, or *UFB Direct*) are special savings accounts that generally pay 20–25 times more than the average national rate on a conventional savings account. The earnings rise is substantial compared to the national average rate for ordinary savings accounts (Karl, 2021).

Suppose you have $5,000 in savings, and the national average annual percentage yield is 0.10% APY. You get $5 in one year. The same $5,000 would yield $100 if you placed it in an account paying 2%.

Money Market Deposit Account

This account may include a debit card, although some institutions do not. Furthermore, a money market account pays interest, just like a savings account, not much, but usually a little beyond a savings account (Ramsey Solutions, 2022).

Keeping your three- to six-month emergency fund in an account of this type makes it accessible but separate from your regular checking account.

Certificate of Deposit (CD)

A CD allows you to make little more money than a checking or savings account and may have a higher risk of losing it all depending on the seller of the CD.

It's, therefore, not a place you choose to invest your money; instead, it's more akin to a certificate of despair. CDs generally return around one percent. Additionally, because inflation increases by roughly 3% annually, you can potentially lose money (Ramsey Solutions, 2022).

CDs have maturity dates—you will be penalized if you withdraw your money before that time. Also, there are short-term, mid-term, and long-term CDs.

The bank offers you a small amount of earned interest when you use a CD to lend them your money. Your interest rate will rise the more you lend them your money.

What Type of Bank Account Am I Using?

If you use internet banking, the nature of your accounts should be apparent when you look them up online. For example, it may read *checking* or *savings* (DeNicola, 2020).

You can ask the teller (cashier) at the bank or phone the bank's customer support if you need access to online banking. The odds are that you are using a savings or checking account. The easiest way to know is if you have a checkbook. If you do, it is a checking account.

Why Do Banks Provide Various Account Types?

Banks provide a variety of accounts because everyone requires a different set of services. Every account type provides a distinct feature. Checking accounts differ from savings accounts, which vary from money market accounts, and so forth.

Which Bank Account is Preferable?

Your needs will determine the most appropriate type of bank account. Most people generally open a checking and savings account when they first open a credit card.

While a checking account is the most adaptable and frequently used for daily transactions, other arrangements offer significant advantages. If you have no banking history at this point in life, open a checking account as soon as you are able to meet the minimum deposit.

Credit Unions and Banks

A credit union requires membership before you may open an account there. They may only allow residents, workers, and worshippers to join (DeNicola, 2020). Credit unions accept applications from just about anyone, but you might need to submit them to a nonprofit organization with a small gift (like $5 or $10).

Credit unions may provide more excellent interest rates on savings accounts and lesser interest rates on credit cards and loans than regular banks, partly because they are nonprofit organizations.

Theoretically, credit unions are permitted to provide share accounts and share draft accounts. Be aware of the terminology; these are equivalent to checking and savings accounts.

Banks are typically for-profit businesses with clients rather than members. You don't need to belong to a specific group to open an account at a bank.

Big banks have locations all over the country or the world. If you travel regularly, a big bank might be more practical than a smaller neighborhood community bank or credit union. Large banks may also provide more cutting-edge technology, such as mobile apps and slick online accounts, compared to smaller banks or credit unions.

You must pay an initial deposit when opening an account, whether at a bank or credit union. A bank or savings account's minimum deposit amount might range from $5 to $25, while some have greater demands (DeNicola, 2020).

UNDERSTANDING INTEREST RATES ON YOUR BANK ACCOUNTS

If you take a loan, you pay interest on it, and it is often stated as a percentage of the loan every year (or the amount borrowed on a credit card).

Your credit union or bank will give you a rate when you save money, which is what determines how much they will loan you. Interest is another word for the cash you receive from saving.

Suppose you deposited $1,000 in a savings account yielding one percent annual interest. After a year, you will have a balance of $1,010 in your account.

Your earnings may differ if the interest rate changes or your savings account's balance shifts when the interest is computed.

You'll make more money over time if you reinvest the money you initially deposited into your savings account and the interest you received. Compounding refers to generating interest on your savings and the total interest accrued over time (Kopp, 2021).

The idea of compound interest is a tool that investors can employ to increase their wealth and savings. Your savings will rise more quickly as interest is added to your balance.

Using the previous $1,000 example. If interest compounds daily, the deposit will increase to $1,010.05 at the year's end. The additional $0.05 seems small.

Yet in ten years, compound interest would cause your $1,000 to increase to $1,105.17. Your investment worth has improved by more than 10% thanks to the daily compounding of 1% interest for ten years.

Consider what might occur if you set aside $100 monthly and add it to the $1,000 down payment.

HOW TO SELECT A BANK THAT SUITS YOUR NEEDS

Your bank should accommodate your financial needs. Every banking establishment has different costs, interest rates, services, and even account kinds. Comparing the crucial specifics to you is helpful (Tarpley, 2022).

Specify bank accounts. Do you want to save money or look for a simple checking account?

Choose the kinds of bank accounts you desire, then search for a bank that provides them.

You'll likely discover several institutions that offer the types of accounts you require. Look for a strategy to focus your search.

Analyze bank products. Some people manage all aspects of their finances through the same organization.

Check to discover if a bank provides any of the following products and services if you want to do more than deposit your money there:

- Credit cards
- Mortgages
- Auto loans
- Financial planning
- Investment accounts

Choose the extra tools you require from your bank. Pick one that provides the services you need.

Examine interest rates. Generally, checking accounts don't offer interest (Tarpley, 2022).

Consider the interest rate while opening an account. You can determine that choosing a bank isn't primarily influenced by the bank's high-interest rate. You may decide on a bank that offers low rates but that you prefer for other factors.

If interest rates are essential to you, pick a provider with reasonable rates.

Find institutions with affordable fees. By establishing a bank account, you would not want to lose money.

Suppose you have three accounts with a company that levies monthly fees for each account. That adds up quickly!

You will most likely seek out a bank that provides one of the following monthly service cost options:

- No fees
- Cancellable fees
- Affordable charges of $3 to $5

You should also be aware of the following fees:

Overdraft. Discover how much a bank will penalize you if you overdraw your checking account.

ATM. What is the size of the ATM network, and would a bank charge a fee if you use an ATM not part of the network?

Find out if the bank will cover any costs incurred by out-of-network ATM service providers.

Excess transaction. Just six withdrawals from money market accounts and savings are permitted monthly without a fee (Tarpley, 2022).

Find out what fees a bank will impose on you if you exceed your limit.

Foreign transaction. If you frequently travel abroad, find out the fees a bank imposes when you use your debit card abroad.

Paper statement. Certain banks can charge you a fee if you register for paper statements.

By signing up for electronic statements, you can avoid paying this fee.

Select the banking option. Choose a bank based on your preference: an online bank or one with physical offices.

If you appreciate being capable of going into a building and chatting with a banker in person, you might choose an offline or static bank. Nevertheless, online banks frequently pay better interest rates and reduced costs.

CHOOSE A SPECIFIC ORGANIZATION

Banks

Banks typically have more locations than credit unions, and they are quicker to adopt new technological advancements in the market (Tarpley, 2022). Some banks provide a more comprehensive range of products, including loans and credit cards.

Credit Unions

Credit unions frequently offer more individualized customer care than banks and provide better savings interest rates.

Banking Platforms

Do you know Chime or Wealthfront? Although these are internet services that provide accounts, they are not banks.

Users can utilize them confidently because of their partner banks' insurance arrangements.

Budgeting tools and high-interest rates are the supplementary benefits of online banking services.

Ensure you can contact your bank. Be sure offices and ATMs are close to your home or place of business if you decide to use a traditional offline bank.

If you frequently travel inside the country, a bank with a sizable branch and ATM network may be what you need to access your money while you're away.

Networks of ATMs exist in online banking. So, confirm that there are free machines nearby.

Observe the details. The bank's federal insurance status should be the first consideration when picking a facility. This implies that your money is secure if something goes wrong and the bank closes.

Read the account disclosures to ensure that you are informed of any potential fees and rules.

Choose the type of service you desire. Your financial requirements may be served by a neighborhood bank, an online-only bank, a not-for-profit organization, or a tech business with a mobile app (Lambarena & Tierney, 2021).

Compare their advantages and disadvantages since they were not all created equally or given equal priority in banking.

- **National banks** offer the broadest selection of accounts and loans in addition to typically top-notch mobile applications and websites.

  Their savings and checking accounts need to be improved. You can be charged a monthly fee if you don't keep a minimum balance. Overdraft costs can be expensive, and savings rates are among the lowest (Lambarena & Tierney, 2021).

- **Regional and neighborhood banks** are well known for their relationship-based banking, particularly regarding mortgages and small business loans.

They might not have the most recent mobile or online banking technology.

- **Credit unions** have conditions for membership. Some only demand a one-time gift to a charity organization, while others require you to work or live in a specific area.

They need to be equipped with the newest technology.

- **Online banks** have the best savings, CD rates, and no monthly fees (Lambarena & Tierney, 2021).

For the most part, mobile apps work well. Most online banks do not have any branches or ATMs that deposit cash.
Some internet banks only provide savings accounts, not checking accounts or the opposite.

Select your favorite features. The greatest of all things won't be found in one place. For instance, finding an online bank with physical locations, a national bank with attractive savings rates, or a credit union with cutting-edge mobile app technology is uncommon.

Think about the services or features you absolutely must have to set expectations.

Contrast comparable alternatives. Check out those banks' reviews to learn more about each financial institution's benefits and drawbacks.

If you already have bank accounts, transferring banks may present some challenges. Nonetheless, it can be profitable, particularly if you benefit from lower prices or better rates.

Everyone can open a bank account; they are not only for people with much money to stash away. To open an account, you need a passport, driver's license, or other state-issued identification cards.

Your checking account can serve as a central location for all your financial transactions, assisting you in keeping track of your payments and adhering to your spending plan.

Every banking establishment has different costs, interest rates, services, and even account kinds. Comparing the specifics that are important to you is, therefore, helpful.

Banks offer tons of perks—flexibility. Security. Affordability. Access to credit. If you don't have a bank account, this might be the appropriate time to open one. Review your favorite financial features and opt for the bank offering them. The next chapter will discuss efficient financial goals.

3

SETTING FINANCIAL GOALS

"Your economic security does not lie in your job; it lies in your own power to produce—to think, to learn, to create, to adapt. That's true financial independence. It's not having wealth, it's having the power to produce wealth." —Stephen Covey

You possess the power to improve your finances. Regardless of your position or title, always remember that your genuine wealth depends on your capacity to continue building it. Achieving anything substantial won't be easy when you have no financial objective. This is why you should set and regularly review your financial goals.

THE IMPORTANCE OF FINANCIAL GOALS

Are you frustrated that you are never successful despite your best efforts to manage your money wisely?

Recession and inflation can sabotage your plans. But, even when things aren't crazy in the market if you don't establish any financial goals, you'll probably still feel like you're going around in circles.

Whatever strategy you have for managing your money is a financial objective (Cruze, 2022). Every part of your life should have goals, but having clear financial objectives can help you put your funds where your priorities are. The decision-making process for your finances can be as complex as selecting a Netflix show to watch.

Consider creating these crucial financial objectives:

Design and follow a budget. Having success with your finances requires having a budget. Budgeting accounts for your revenue and outgoing expenses. Instead of figuring out where your money went, you're telling it where to go.

Save for emergencies. Job loss. Car troubles. Unplanned medical expenses. If you have enough money saved up, you can be ready for any financial issues that may arise.

When you have an emergency fund, you'll feel secure knowing you have the funds to handle unpredictable circumstances.

Eliminate debt. Debt holds you back rather than advancing you. If all your money goes toward payments, it's impossible to prosper financially (Cruze, 2022). Start taking your debt repayment seriously if you have any.

Save for retirement. Imagine your dream retirement for a moment.

- Do you want to take your grandchildren to Disney World every Christmas?
- Do you want to start a new pastime or travel to a different state with your partner once every three months?

Whatever your future goals, you'll need wise retirement investing to make them a reality. Consider setting aside 15% of your family's net income for retirement.

Minimize spending and improve saving. Your spending habits should be deliberate. Set a budget and adhere to it.

- Use coupons.
- Understand when to say no, even to yourself.

- Plan your menu—most Americans overspend on food (Cruze, 2022).

Significance of Having Financial Purposes

You may manage your money more strategically if you have a goal in mind. Every choice you make impacts your financial situation.

Suppose you spend $25 on lattes weekly, up to $100 monthly!

The potential of compound interest may enable you to turn $100 invested each month for five years into $8,000.

You're drinking a whole session of your kids' college classes!

Consider what would happen if you made an even longer-term investment of $100 monthly for 15 years. Your savings from lattes might reach almost $45,000.

And suppose you put your money in investments for 30 years? Your coffee budget can increase to more than $280,000.

Show financial destination. We have the power to improve the quality of our lives. Making the proper judgments becomes more straightforward when you have a goal in mind (Money Nuggets, n.d.).

Reveal saving target. What amount of savings and investments are necessary for you to reach your financial objectives? You may place a number on your aspirations by defining and quantifying financial goals.

Expose strategies. It can be sufficient to save a little additional money each month if your financial goals are reasonably small.

Suppose your long-term goals include getting a house and retiring early. To accumulate money and reach your financial objectives more quickly, you may have to raise your income, reduce spending, and invest.

Define career preferences. If your objectives are ambitious, consider how much vacation time to take (or what to do) to boost your chances of improving your income. You might have to give up your nine-to-five job to launch a business to achieve some financial goals.

Facilitate concentration. Take an image of your objectives and post it near your desk—this helps you resist spending money on something you don't need. It reminds you of the purpose of your extra labor.

Support tool discovery. *Google Play* and *Apple Store* have many accessible (and affordable) financial tools. For example, you can invest using *Wealthify* and save through *Plum*.

Encourage a feeling of triumph. Praise yourself for starting your new financial path and overcoming the first obstacle. You don't have to go it alone; individuals seeking assistance have a much higher chance of success (Money Nuggets, n.d.).

HOW TO SET EFFICIENT FINANCIAL GOALS WITH THE SMART FORMULA

A smart objective is precise, clear, attainable, objective, and time-bound. It involves setting a clear financial goal with a workable plan.

Consider the scenario where you wish to pay off your $5,000 credit card debt by the end of 2024. You must set aside about $420 per month and refrain from making any transactions with the card for the next 12 months (Fullerton Markets, 2021).

That's a more concise strategy than merely stating your intention to pay off your obligations. A creative financial goal transforms a general approach into something that can be completed within a set timeframe.

A SMART Goal Example

Let's say you want to create additional or many sources of income. You want your financial situation to be solid enough to withstand any turbulence, such as a pandemic, a recession, or a loss of employment.

How would you formulate a clear objective for this?

Respond to these five Ws to develop a specific approach.

What? I want to invest.

Why? I want to generate more revenue and attain financial security.

Where? I will invest my extra funds after meeting all my costs.

Who? I will watch webinars and take advice from mentors.

Which. Unexpected costs could soar. You might have to pay for your medical care if you get sick.

Your objectives take on a solid form rather than remaining merely an abstract idea by responding to these questions. You'll understand the reason for your actions and the difficulties you must prepare for.

You might be wondering about gauging your development. Reviewing the information below may help.

- What percentage of income growth are you hoping to achieve? **$10,000.**

- How much cash are you able to set aside monthly? **$900**.

Do a check-in once every three months. Based on your investment activity, your equity should grow by at least 3%, with your initial capital being $2,700. You might be capable of reaching your objective quicker than you anticipated if you reinvest what you make.

Will this strategy work? You can easily reach your goal of $10,000 in one year if you contribute $900 to your monthly savings account. When investing in stocks or currencies, you might achieve your goal sooner if your financial choices result in higher gains.

- Is your objective consistent with your life's plan?

Your strategy is relevant if your desire for many sources of income resolves or improves your financial situation. The same is valid if your goal for this year is to make more informed financial decisions.

- How long until you reach your objective?

Your calculations suggest you can achieve your goal in 12 months. The deadline will help you stay focused on your goal and hold yourself accountable.

Here's how to set efficient financial goals using the SMART formula.

Create a precise goal. Start by investing for retirement or increasing your savings. These are fantastic starting ideas, but with a specific target, goals are easier to achieve (Waugh, 2022).

How much of each paycheck would you like to set aside?

How much money would you like to put aside for retirement?

Defining them further can help to make these objectives more precise:

I want to transfer $100 from each paycheck to a high-yield savings account.

I want to contribute a percentage of every paycheck I receive to my 401(k) account to save money for retirement.

The clarity, motivation, and ease of achieving specific financial goals are improved.

Measure your progress. If you are saving for emergencies, specify the amount to save weekly or monthly. By doing so, you can determine whether you're on track and what has to be done to reach your goal.

Make your objective measurable by specifying your contribution amount if you have a retirement goal.

Make your objective feasible. Setting up automatic contributions is one of the finest methods to make your investment goal more attainable when investing for retirement.

You'll resist the urge to spend the funds elsewhere if you consistently put funds into your retirement account.

Cutting back on unnecessary expenditures and looking for methods to boost your income are two approaches to making your financial objectives more attainable.

Set realistic targets. Suppose your income is meager. Establishing a savings target for a $100,000 luxurious wedding in 2 years would be challenging, if not impossible. Plan your objective on what you can afford.

The average price of a wedding event and reception in 2021 was $28,000. You might reduce your spending to that amount. Alternatively, postpone your nuptials for a few years to save for a bigger feasible wedding (Waugh, 2022).

Maintain a timeline. Divide a goal into more manageable chunks, such as saving $1 million by the time you retire. Saving $7,000 by the end of the year for retirement is a timeline goal.

If you want to create a SMART loan payoff strategy, you could choose a time frame—say, two or three years—to be debt-free.

WHAT TO CONSIDER WHEN DECIDING ON YOUR FINANCIAL GOALS

Without a clear goal in mind, you run the risk of going overboard with your spending. Then, when you need funds for unforeseen expenses, you won't have enough.

It's possible to fall victim to a never-ending cycle of credit card debt and believe you will never have enough money to secure enough insurance to protect yourself against some of life's biggest threats.

Short-term goals. Clearing credit card balances and establishing reserve money are examples of short-term objectives. These plans build confidence by preparing you for longer-term, more ambitious goals.

Mid-term goals connect short-term and long-term objectives. A mid-term aim is to purchase disability income insurance or life insurance. The purchase of a car and improving a home are other mid-term objectives.

Long-term goals. Many people point to retirement savings when discussing long-term objectives.

Financial experts recommend contributing between 10% and 15% of your income to a tax-advantaged retirement account (Fontinelle, 2022).

Determining the amount you need for retirement is necessary to ensure you save enough.

Avoid these errors when establishing your financial objectives:

Separating financial objectives. Connect your financial decisions to your goals. For example, your ability to save or invest will determine whether your retirement objective is successful (Abraham, 2018). You should skip some shorter-term ambitions to reach crucial objectives like saving for emergencies.

Investing without matching objectives. By investing savings in equities products to receive better returns, you risk jeopardizing a short-term aim if the market declines and your assets lose value.

A product that doesn't provide a consistent income stream or permit constant withdrawals is inadequate for storing money for recurring monthly education costs.

Not setting benchmarks. Declaring a requirement without identifying the models to achieve it leads nowhere—you won't get the desired outcomes.

Let's say your five-year goal is to save up the deposit for a house. You won't have a plan to strive for if you don't quantify the amount needed.

Defining goals aids in progress tracking. To make it simpler to track your progress and make a big, long-term goal appear more manageable and attainable, break it down into smaller, more immediate objectives (Abraham, 2018).

Disregarding the significance of flexibility. Be willing to adjust your goals. If your assets have been used to pay for your child's sports coaching, you might want to consider delaying your retirement. When current objectives become obsolete, you must replace them with fresh ones.

Planning procedure without including review. Making assumptions about various aspects is a necessary step in goal-setting. You make a cost estimate for achieving the target based on current costs and projected inflation.

You account for your income and capacity to limit costs when calculating savings. You chose investments based on the market's anticipated performance.

Your goal will have to be altered if one or more of these presumptions needs to be corrected.

ADJUSTING FINANCIAL GOALS

Working for your financial objectives is a terrific, proactive step, but if your goals are too lofty, you risk disappointing yourself and straying from your purpose CCS, n.d.).

Financial objectives, as well as the path to reaching them, could be more manageable. What can you do if your ambitions seem unattainable?

Identify the problem. Are you aiming to pay off hefty credit card debt within a year? Take a seat, be honest, and carefully calculate the numbers.

You must realize that your objective is unachievable if it requires you to make debt payments or save money that is more than your income.

Determine strategies for overcoming the obstacle. If your goals seem unattainable, fix the barriers keeping you from progressing in your financial future.

Your financial goal shouldn't be stagnant. To make sure you're still moving in the right direction toward your objectives, you should regularly assess your plans.

Depending on your unique position, review your finances at least once a year and whenever something significant occurs in your financial or personal condition (WFP, n.d.).

Consider these things when reviewing your finances.

Objectives. Your goals may have changed, or you might have set new ones as you reached your old ones.

Notions. You may discover that your earlier presumptions could be more pessimistic or realistic. Your predictions may need to be corrected because it is difficult to foresee the future.

Revenue. When your work value rises and your assets increase, your income will change—hopefully for the better (WFP, n.d.).

Payments. This will change as your circumstances change.

Assets. Amend your schedule of assets to reflect changes in prices and acquisitions.

Liabilities. Progress in lowering expenses should allow you to stay informed about your payments.

Cash flow management. Consider the adjustments when revising your strategy to see how they affect your capacity to achieve your objectives.

Contingency preparation. You might think you have enough money to handle an emergency, but you should double-check.

Protective resources. Reevaluate your needs in light of your attitudes, resources, and obligations to your family.

Settling debt. If your strategy is solid, results should start showing up quickly.

Future investing. Reevaluate your strategy for wealth growth, considering your attitude toward risk. Rebalance your investments because some will have increased in value more quickly than others.

Evaluate effect. When an unexpected expense arises, determine its impact on your spending strategy. For example, estimate how long it will take to pay off an unexpected medical expenditure.

Pay the distinction. Reducing your spending can assist you in making up for a shortage. You may also increase your income by taking on a second part-time job or contract position; so far it doesn't negatively impact your current job (Wells Fargo, n.d.).

While postponing your objective might not be the best course of action, it might be the most practical. The important thing is to make every effort to limit setbacks. Even if you cannot save the total amount, you should find ways to raise your monthly savings to attain your goal sooner.

Money was not a concern for Kyle and Lauren Mochizuki when getting married in 2009; they just wanted to enjoy themselves. They accrued liabilities of $266,000 due to a month-long adventure in Europe and the funding of a mortgage, two high value vehicles, and holidays.

To ensure that cash was in their accounts, Kyle had to carefully manage his two automobile payments, which were ten months behind schedule. Debt-related stress had already started overwhelming him. So, after talking with Lauren, the couple made the decision to begin paying down their liabilities.

Kyle and Lauren were more committed, taking on different work schedules, meal planning, and canceling memberships. Their finances improved as they crossed off obligations and settled accounts—they were left with just the mortgage outstanding.

Since the couple had no kids during the period, they decided to be debt-free before having a child. They paid off their loan after thirty-three months and welcomed a child a year after.

Every part of your life should have goals, but having clear financial objectives can help you put your funds where your priorities are.

Recession and inflation can sabotage your plans. But, even when things aren't crazy in the market, if you don't establish any financial goals, you'll likely still feel like you're going in circles.

Your strategy is relevant if your desire for many sources of income resolves or improves your financial situation. The same is valid if your goal for this year is to make more informed financial decisions.

Goals give you something to aim for—individuals with no objectives have nothing to achieve. If you're setting financial goals, ensuring they are practical and motivating helps. The next chapter will discuss the importance of budgeting and saving money.

4

BUDGETING AND SAVING

Budgeting aids short and long-term financial planning. It keeps you within a predetermined spending limit. It grants you the ability to control your finances. Tracking the money you have left over following all your spending ensures you are not getting into debt. Establishing attainable financial objectives helps you start the budget-making process (Great Lakes, n.d.).

After setting your financial goals, it is time to figure out how to achieve them. In most cases, the first step towards these goals is saving money. To save money and efficiently manage your income, you should create a budget that helps you keep track of expenses and your savings progress.

WHAT IS A BUDGET?

A budget is a plan for spending money. It projects your income and expenses for a specific timeframe, usually a month (Schwahn, 2020). Making a detailed list of costs or concentrating on a few areas can be part of budgeting. Some people favor handwriting their budgets, while others utilize a budgeting app or spreadsheet. There is no ideal budget; what is effective for someone may not be for another.

Budgets have three categories—surplus, balance, and deficit (Ganti, 2022). A surplus budget indicates that profits are projected. It implies that you earn more than you spend. With a balanced budget, your income and expenses are equal. A deficit budget indicates that spending is higher than income.

Lack of funds may prevent some people from tracking their financial flows from one month to another. Still, everyone may create and use a budget. Maintaining a budget is more complicated than it seems—that credit card is still calling your name, and you might think budgets are boring. So, how do you budget effortlessly?

Focus on your ultimate objective. Consider your desired future and remember that adhering to your budget will assist you in achieving it.

Eliminate the choices making you splurge. Ditch impulse buying and create obstacles that make you pause and check if a purchase is essential.

- Remove yourself from retailers' email lists.
- If there are any subscriptions you are not using, cancel them.
- Delete your saved payment information from your favorite online stores so you don't just click to order.

Seek help. If nobody in your team uses a budget, look for others who share your viewpoints. You may also establish accountability by discussing issues and staying out of temptation with your thrifty friends.

Compensate yourself. Reward yourself after sticking to your budget for a month. Modest ones are beneficial, like a party with friends or a concert.

Be enlightened. Instead of choosing the usual course of immediate results, which always results in overspending and debt, learn to control your finances. Ask your money-savvy acquaintances for guidance and recommendations from individuals who are successful with their money.

Curb potential disaster. Be bold and ask creditors for payment arrangements or bill extensions. Making partial or late payments worsens your debt; late fees also lower your credit score.

Prioritize debt refund. Go through your bills to determine what you must pay first. Establish a payment plan that aligns with your paydays. If some of your expenses are past due, give yourself some catch-up time.

Contact the bill collectors to determine how much you can pay immediately to resume your path to success. Inform them of the efforts you are taking to catch up. Don't merely pledge to spend the whole amount later; be upfront about how much you can afford to pay.

Reduce spending. Categorize your expenditure so that you may make modifications using online banking and budgeting tools.

- Make the required adjustments after better understanding where your funds flow.
- Start all budget cuts with things you wouldn't miss.
- If you discover that ingredients are ruined before consumption, you might reduce your fresh food purchases.
- Cook food at home more frequently rather than eating out or ordering takeout.

Bargain credit card charges. Call the card company and request a discount on the annual percentage rates (APR). The company may grant your request if you have an excellent credit history.

Seek additional earnings. Consider strategies to improve your income, such as working extra hours, taking on a second job, or starting a side business.

Why Do You Need a Budget?

Following a budget when starting your financial path will help you develop good money management skills. Creating a budget may balance your income, savings, and expenses. It also directs your spending and assists you in achieving your financial objectives.

Maintain focus on goals. A budget compels you to set goals, save money, monitor progress, and realize your aspirations (Bell, 2022). You can make a plan to reach your objective by using a budget to track your income and outgoing funds.

Prevent splurge. Consumers spend far too much money they don't have, and credit cards are entirely to blame. Nowadays, those who misuse and overuse credit cards frequently only recognize their overspending once they are buried in debt. You're more likely to avoid this situation if you make and adhere to a budget.

Happier retirement. You can accumulate a comfortable nest egg with monthly contributions to your retirement account.

Emergency support. Situations like being laid off, having an expensive emergency home repair, or being ill can cause severe financial hardship. An emergency fund can be helpful in these circumstances (Bell, 2022).

Expose poor money habits. Using a budget, you can reevaluate your spending patterns and realign your financial objectives. Looking at your spending, you might discover eating out costs more than preparing food at home. Reviewing your budget will enable you to make worthwhile adjustments.

Boost savings. Controlling your finances becomes simple when using a budget. You determine what gets spent or saved. Since following a budget helps trim needless payments, you have more cash to save.

Ease major purchases. Having a budget prepares you for a significant investment. For example, saving towards a big purchase requires a plan—a budget.

Curb stress. If you have to rack your brain before discovering where your money goes, you may experience financial stress. Having a budget is a way to avoid this situation.

COMMON BUDGETING PITFALLS

What could I improve at making or maintaining a budget?

Instead of stressing about your financial status, investing time in learning about money blunders you might not even be aware of can be beneficial.

Forgetting to prepare for costs. While budgeting for fixed payments may be straightforward, variable prices may require a complex approach. Suppose you budget $50 for dining out. You may spend more if you frequently eat out more than once a week (Lockert, 2022).

Failing to track payments. How would you know whether you are adhering to your budget if you set one but don't keep track of your spending?

Not evaluating the budget. Revise and adjust your budget regularly. Focus areas may include transitional periods (such as those following a layoff) and instances where you go under or over your budget.

Overlooking budgeting because of varying earnings. If you work in a commission-based position, your monthly income is unpredictable. Regardless of your income, the 50/30/20 budget may work well for you because it gives you percentages to use as a guide (Lockert, 2022).

Refusing to document a budget. Budgeting is a chore that, despite your best attempts, you cannot finish in your thoughts. With written funding, you avoid exceeding your monthly spending limit (Financial Bank, n.d.). Even if you believe you understand your budget correctly, there will inevitably be expenditures that change or are overlooked.

Establishing unattainable budgeting plans. Setting too low a saving objective could lead to future financial strain. Raising your goals too high may lead to budgetary disappointment. Consider your options carefully and try your best to stick to your budget.

Failing to monitor one-time payments. You must record one-time expenses to ensure your budget is accurate. Budgeting month-to-month and noting all unusual spending on your calendar will help you efficiently avoid this error.

Downplaying emergency payments. Your budget may only improve if you account for unexpected costs. You risk increasing your debt if you don't prepare for these unforeseen costs.

Not allocating funds for fun. While having fun can be spontaneous, you can prepare for the associated costs.

Think about including one or two leisure days in your spending plan. In this way, you can spend a day or a weekend away with friends without later experiencing financial difficulty.

Feeling frustrated because the budget didn't seem to be working. If you have not seen any improvements in your finances, your budget probably needs more time to work. Keep attempting to stick to a strict budget. Keep tracking and maintaining a realistic spending pattern (Financial Bank, n.d.).

Not minimizing costs. Increasing your income to cover your increased spending may only sometimes work. Cutting costs is necessary to ensure that you stay within your budget.

Forgetting to mend budgeting delinquencies. If you struggle to make your budget function, step back and analyze each issue.

- Do you spend too much money each month?
- Do you keep your budget the same?
- Have you found a suitable budgeting strategy?

Failing to automate debt payments. You want to meet the deadline because you didn't account for late fines or other expenses. As you remove the pressure of remembering to pay, you also eliminate the chance that you'll fail to pay your bills (Financial Bank, n.d.).

BUILDING YOUR BUDGET

A budget gives you financial control and simplifies saving funds for your objectives. You can create a budget by following these steps.

Compute your net revenue. Your net earnings are your salary minus tax and employer-sponsored benefits like health insurance and retirement plans (BOA, n.d.).

Monitor your expenses. Classify your purchases to spot what you spend money on and payments to cut to raise savings. Write out your monthly fees, including rent or mortgage, utilities, and auto payments. List your variable expenses, which include groceries, gas, and entertainment. Using a smartphone app or budgeting spreadsheets, track your everyday spending.

Establish attainable objectives. Although your goals can be flexible, knowing what they are can inspire you to keep to your spending plan. For instance, if you know you're saving for a vacation, it might be simpler to reduce spending.

Create a strategy. Use your fixed and variable expense list to estimate your spending over the next few months. Then contrast that with your priorities and net income. Consider establishing explicit, attainable spending targets for every expense category.

Modify your purchases to maintain your budget. Can we see a film at home instead of going to the movies? Examine your monthly payment expenses more closely if you've already adjusted your spending on wants.

Check your fixed expenses for adjustments if the figures don't add up. For example, you may find a better auto or homeowner insurance deal if you search around. Consider your options carefully before making such choices because they include significant trade-offs.

Conduct an ongoing budget analysis. You might get a raise, trim spending, or opt for another goal after attaining the previous one. Updating your budget helps align your finances with your objectives.

Learn the budgeting approach. Your budget should address your needs, part of your wants, and future emergencies. Use internet tools for conserving money and keeping track of your spending. Automate as much as possible to ensure that the funds for a particular use arrive with the least effort on your side.

Create a budget worksheet. Find out your net income first, then assess your current spending. Apply the

50/30/20 rule—50%, 30%, and 20% of your income to your needs, wants, and savings (or debt reimbursement), respectively (O'Shea & Schwahn, 2022).

Manage the spending plan. Categorize your costs after reviewing your account statements and maintain consistency in your tracking. Allocate approximately 50% of gross earnings for necessities. You might need to temporarily remove money from your "wants" category if your needs exceed the 50% threshold.

Reserve 30% of your earnings for wants. Are trips to restorative spas (with advice for a massage) desired or necessary? How about purchasing organic food? Individuals' wants vary. Spend 20% of your after-tax income on debt repayment, saving for the future, and emergency savings. Consider your overall financial situation; doing so may need you to alternate between saving and paying off debt to achieve your most urgent objectives.

How frequently should you evaluate your spending plan? Set out budget reviews at least once monthly, although many people favor doing this weekly or after getting paid (BTG, n.d.).

WHAT PROPORTION OF YOUR SALARY SHOULD YOU SAVE?

Your recommended savings rate is based on your unique, long-term saving goals. If it is retirement, consider setting aside 10 to 15% of your salary. Your emergency fund could be three to nine months of regular living expenditures. One more general guideline is to save at least 20% of your income (Pant, n.d.). Embracing these methods can help you save early and frequently.

Automate your savings. Set up direct payments to automatically transfer a proportion of your salary to a savings account.

Take advantage of retirement funds. For retirement programs like 401(k)s and 403(b)s, many employers provide matching contributions, which implies they will match any payments you make up to a specific percentage (Muller, 2023). This may be a simple approach to increase the funds you put aside for retirement from each paycheck by two times.

Deposit funds into numerous accounts. Setting up separate accounts for long- and short-term objectives might make it easier to monitor progress and guarantee that all deadlines are reached. For example, opening an emergency fund account might provide the comfort of knowing money is always set aside if something unexpected arises.

Maximize your savings strategy. Money market accounts and other low-risk products like CDs are secure places to park your money where you can gradually earn income. Ensure you thoroughly read the terms and conditions before selecting an investment option. Hence, you know how much risk you're accepting and what kind of return you may anticipate. Before investing in any retirement plan, speak with a financial counselor or accountant to learn more about the types of deductions that are accessible and how they'll impact your entire financial situation.

BUILDING AN EMERGENCY FUND

Emergency savings help manage unexpected needs such as job loss, auto repair, and medical bills. In general, unanticipated invoices or payments that are not a standard component of your monthly spending can be covered by your emergency funds, whether big or small (CFPB, n.d.).

Without reserves, even a small financial shock could be detrimental. If it results in debt, it might have long-term effects. Those with difficulty recovering from a financial panic may have fewer savings to assist them in preparing for a future emergency. They might rely on loans or credit cards, resulting in debt that is typically more difficult to pay off. They might also use other savings, such as retirement accounts, to pay for these expenses.

Consider the most frequent unforeseen expense type you've encountered in the past and the amount of those expenses. This helps you determine how much you'd set aside. The simplest ways to get started include managing your cash flow and saving some tax refunds. Make sure this money is secure, easily accessible, and located in a position where you won't be tempted to use it for things other than emergencies. Consider these options when saving for emergencies.

Financial institutions. A specific account where you can hold and manage these funds may make sense if you've opened an account with a credit union or bank.

Prepaid card. Deposit the funds using a prepaid card. Prepaid cards are not affiliated with any financial institution, and you cannot spend more than the amount on them (CFPB, n.d.).

Cash. You may keep some money on hand for unplanned expenses at home or with a dependable relative or friend. Remember to establish rules for an emergency or unforeseen expense before reaching out for the funds.

> Budgeting aids short and long-term financial planning. It keeps you within a predetermined spending limit. It grants you the ability to control your finances.
>
> Following a budget when starting your financial path will help you develop good money management skills. Creating a budget may balance your income, savings, and expenses. It also directs your spending and assists you in achieving your financial objectives.
>
> Instead of stressing about your financial status, investing time in learning about money blunders you might not even be aware of can be beneficial.

Whether you want to track your money, manage your finances, or accomplish your financial objectives, establishing and maintaining a budget helps. The upcoming chapter will discuss credit, credit scores, and credit cards.

5

MANAGING CREDIT

Creditors use credit scores to assess a debtor's creditworthiness or the probability that they can repay their loan in full and on time. According to Experian, if your credit score is 800, you have an excellent credit score. According to a FICO assessment, only 23% of creditworthy people have scores of 800 or higher (Paul, 2022).

For many people, credit can be considered a blessing and a curse. It can be highly convenient in unforeseen circumstances where cash is needed quickly. Many people, however, need help to handle credit responsibly and end up in debt. This is why you should know exactly how credit works before getting into financial trouble.

WHAT IS CREDIT?

Credit is your capacity to obtain funds on credit, as well as goods or services, with the expectation that you will make payment later. Whether you are granted credit by a lender, a retailer, or a service provider depends on how confident they are in your ability to repay the money you borrowed plus any associated finance charges.

Your history of borrowing money and repaying it is what creditors in the US normally consider when providing credit. *Experian, TransUnion,* and *Equifax*—three independent credit bureaus—generate the credit reports that describe your credit history. Banks, credit card companies, credit unions, and other creditors voluntarily report your borrowing and repayment history to the credit bureaus (Akin, 2019).

Your credit report comprises the number of credit card accounts, the amount on each card, and your overall debt balance. It also highlights your borrowing history, including the total amount borrowed and the amount you have already paid back. Studying your credit statement helps creditors know whether you paid your bills on time, after the due date, or missed them altogether. The report also contains information about your financial setbacks, including bankruptcy, repossessions of vehicles, and mortgage foreclosure.

Creditors frequently use a three-digit figure known as a credit score as the initial step in determining their lending decisions. Credit cards have four types—revolving, charge, service, and installment credit cards.

Revolving credit. With revolving credit, there is a cap on how much you may borrow or charge. You must make a minimum monthly payment and pay the entire amount owed or any part of it. In the event of a partial payment, you will carry the remaining balance forward. Most credit cards fall under revolving credit (Akin, 2019).

Charge cards. You can use these cards like people use revolving credit cards but cannot carry a balance. Instead, you are required to pay off all charges in full each month.

Service credit. Your agreements with companies who supply services like internet and electricity are all credit contracts. Some businesses agree to give you their services monthly in exchange for payment that you make later.

Installment credit. A loan you accept to repay over a predetermined time in a series of equal payments every month (plus fees and interest) is an installment credit.

Installment credit includes mortgages, auto loans, and student loans.

You must have good credit to borrow funds for large expenditures like a car or home. Many card issuers save their most alluring rewards cards for those with excellent credit. When considering whether or not to rent you an apartment or how much of a security deposit to demand, landlords may examine your credit.

Insurance companies may take your credit ratings into account when calculating your rates. Utility providers may run a credit check before choosing whether to open an account for you or allow you to borrow equipment. Potential employers may use data from credit reports to decide whether to hire a job applicant.

Credit vs Debt

Credit and debt differ because credit allows you to buy something now and pay it off later. In contrast, debt is the total amount you owe at any time. You have credit but no debt if you haven't used your credit card (Debt.org, n.d.).

CREDIT SCORES, REPORTS, AND FREEZES

A credit rating ranges from 300 to 850. Creditors use the score to determine your financial risk or whether you can repay your loans on time. Your credit ratings are one consideration for creditors and lenders when deciding whether to authorize you for a new account. Your credit scores might also affect the rate of interest and other conditions of any debts or different credit accounts you are eligible for (Equifax, n.d.).

Loan arrangements are often more favorable for debtors with higher credit ratings, which could result in cheaper payments and interest costs for the account. Depending on their businesses, creditors, and lenders may utilize several credit scores. For example, if you're purchasing a car, an auto loan lender may use a credit score that gives more weight to your payment history. These elements determine your credit score:

Payment. Your payment history determines 35% of your score—this displays your payment history, including whether you pay bills on time, how frequently you miss payments, how many days you pay bills past their due dates, and how recently missed payments have occurred.

Lenders often report late payments that are more than 30 days overdue, which affects your credit scores. Different variables come into play, such as how far back you are on a given bill, how many accounts exhibit late payments, and whether you have kept the accounts current. Your credit score will increase as your percentage of on-time payments rises. You damage your credit score each time you make a late payment.

Debt. 30% of your score is based on how much obligation you have from loans and credit cards—this is determined by the total sum you owe, the variety and quantity of accounts you possess, and the debt ratio to your available credit (Wells Fargo, n.d.). Smaller amounts may boost your credit score if you make on-time payments. Your credit score may temporarily decline if you take out new loans with minimal payment history. Still, it may rise if you take out loans that are nearly paid off since they have a satisfactory payment history.

Duration. 15% of your creditworthiness is determined by the length of your credit record. Your creditworthiness will improve the sooner you maintain on-time repayments. While analyzing creditworthiness, credit-scoring algorithms frequently consider your credit's overall age. Consider keeping your accounts open and active as a result.

Account. Your score is 10% based on the kinds of accounts you have. Various accounts, such as installment loans, house loans, retail cards, and credit cards, can boost your credit score (Wells Fargo, n.d.).

Activity. The last 10% is made up of recent credit activity. Current account closures or entries may suggest potential financial problems and lower your score.

How Soon After Establishing an Account Do You Receive a Credit Rating?

Your credit report's data is used to calculate your credit score. So, you usually need 3 to 6 months' worth of credit activity before generating one (White, 2022).

What is the Use of Credit Statements?

Credit reports are used by creditors to decide whether to provide you with credit or approve a loan. The reports also play a role in determining how much interest they will impose on you. Potential employers, insurance, and landlords might also view your credit report. You won't be able to predict which credit report a lender or employer will use to examine your credit (USAGCR, n.d.).

What Justifies Checking Your Credit Rating?

Regularly verify the accuracy of your financial and personal information by checking your credit reports. Checking to see if any bogus accounts have been opened in your name also helps. Take action to have any mistakes in your credit report fixed if you uncover any.

How Can You Access Your Credit Information?

You are eligible for a free annual credit analysis from the credit reporting bureaus on AnnualCreditReport.com. Many people are struggling financially as a result of the COVID-19 outbreak. Until December 2023, you can obtain free credit reports weekly to help you stay in charge of your money (USAGCR, n.d.).

Credit Freeze

You can limit who can access your credit report by putting a freeze on it—this is crucial after an identity theft or data breach because someone can use your details to open new credit accounts. Creditors cannot access your credit record if it has been frozen and will likely reject false applications.

Write a letter challenging any mistakes you notice in your credit report and any necessary supporting proof. After that, please mail it to the relevant credit reporting agency (CRA) and the company that supplied the false data. Credit card and bank firms are some of these suppliers. The CRA and the organization that provided the information will correct your credit record.

You have a reporting period of seven years, or until the statute of limitations expires, to disclose information concerning a lawsuit or judgment against you. Unpaid tax liens can remain on your record for 15 years and bankruptcy for up to 10 years (USAGCR, n.d.).

BUILDING AND IMPROVING YOUR CREDIT SCORE

There might be quick strategies to raise your credit score if it is lower than you would want. You can add up to 100 points rather rapidly, depending on what's keeping it down. Credit bureaus use your credit reports to compute your credit scores. Although scoring models differ, the following factors are often taken into account.

Payment. Missed or late payments may significantly impact your credit score.

Credit utilization. Divide your outstanding credit by the total credit available in your accounts to compute your credit utilization rate. Lenders frequently prefer credit usage rates of at least 30% (Equifax, n.d.). Lenders may view having accessible credit as a favorable indicator because it shows that you're just using the credit you need.

Most lenders prefer to see established credit lines—this implies that it's important to keep credit accounts active (even if you aren't using them), as removing them can result in a shorter credit history overall.

Credit mix. Your diverse portfolio of accounts, such as your credit cards, mortgages, and student loans, is your credit mix. Lenders may assume you are familiar with the basics of credit if you maintain variety and good payment history.

Debt. Your current debt equals all outstanding balances on all your lines of credit. Try to eliminate all of your balances each month (if possible). By doing this, you can keep your debt from growing and demonstrate your ability to make timely payments to creditors.

Examine your credit reports from the three national consumer reporting agencies (*Experian, TransUnion,* and *Equifax*). Check to discover any outstanding amounts and pay off as many past-due loans as possible. Pay off your bills on schedule and avoid making late payments whenever you can. If you have trouble making timely payments, consider setting up alerts to remind you to pay or using automatic payments for your accounts.

Have a credit usage rate of 30% or less. You can lower your utilization rate by asking your credit card company to increase your limits. Only open a few new accounts because requesting additional lines of credit can harm your credit score. Hold onto previous accounts—avoid canceling any previously paid-off accounts, especially if you no longer use them, while trying to raise your score.

How Much Time is Required for Improvements to Your Credit Rating to Be Visible?

Different drawbacks require different levels of effort to overcome. One late payment would be easier to recover from than a foreclosure, which might take longer. Insufficient information, such as late payments, often lasts seven years on your credit report. Recall that it takes time and work to raise your credit score. Your credit score will only magically improve if you choose a one-size-fits-all approach (Equifax, n.d.).

How is Credit Established or Built?

Your payment history may impact your credit score. Before raising your credit score, try to have a more extended credit history. Embracing these tips may help build and establish your credit.

Secured credit. Protected credit cards are the ideal starting point because they assist users in building credit histories. You must make an upfront deposit for a secure card, often equal to your proposed credit limit. Like every other credit card, the card functions and timely payments help establish a good credit history.

Student credit. You can also consider getting a student credit card if you meet the requirements. Your school enrollment needs to be verified.

Ratified user. To begin growing credit without applying for a payment gateway, ask your parents or spouse to put you as an account holder on their bank cards. You wouldn't own the account; instead, you would be an authorized user and benefit from timely payments.

Co-signer. A co-signer is an individual who voluntarily agrees to assume legal responsibility for repaying debt, such as an automobile or school loan, if the borrower cannot make the loan's agreed-upon payments (Equifax, n.d.). You could obtain better loan conditions or be approved for a loan that you otherwise wouldn't be able to get with the help of a co-signer.

WHAT YOU SHOULD KNOW ABOUT CREDIT CARDS

If you use your credit cards longer than you can pay back each month, you risk getting into debt. Yet, when used responsibly, a credit card can be an effective financial instrument and a vital component of developing credit so you can realize your future aspirations, like purchasing a home or automobile. Credit cards can also access card advantages and earn purchase rewards (Hoffman, 2023).

A credit card is just a modest loan from the issuing bank. Your account will be given a credit limit when the bank authorizes your request for a credit card. This credit limit represents the most the bank will permit you to spend using the card. Various factors determine your credit card limit, including income, obligations, credit history, etc.

Credit card transactions are handled through payment providers. They are responsible for ensuring the merchant is paid for the trade and that your card provider invoices you for the transaction. If you pay off your credit card balance, you will have more accessible credit for future purchases (Hoffman, 2023).

Credit vs. debit cards. A linked bank account is used to deduct the price of the product you are purchasing via a debit card. You are spending money that has been placed into a bank account when paying with a debit card.

Using a credit card lets you make an immediate purchase and last payment. You can spread out the expense of your credit card account if you cannot pay it off in full. Most credit card companies charge interest on delinquent balances, but for some people, the freedom to carry debt when necessary outweighs the additional interest fees.

Credit cards are typically the more secure financial tool, although both cards have safeguards to help prevent fraud. Zero fraud liability is a benefit that almost all popular credit cards have, which means you are not liable for paying back illegal or fraudulent charges (Hoffman, 2023).

Settling debt monthly to prevent high-interest charges. If you cannot clear your balance at once, try to make a lower payment (but it must be within the required minimum payment). Any sum on your statement that is still unpaid will start to accrue interest; however, the lower the balance, the less interest you'll pay.

Configure credit card spending notifications. Install the mobile application from your credit card issuer and log in to your account. Go to your alert or notification choices for your credit card. You can find this under "Settings" for some programs. From the list of options, choose the alerts you want to configure.

Set a monthly budget cap for your credit card. A credit limit is the ultimate maximum amount a lender will permit a borrower to take out on a line of credit or credit card. You can incur a fee or have other unfavorable effects if you exceed the credit limit the card issuer sets.

Reduce your credit use rate. Your credit usage is just the percentage of your accessible credit that you are currently using. It is calculated by dividing your overall credit limit by the sum of your credit card balances. Consider making a payment or using another card if you are about to use 30% of the available credit on one of your cards (O'Shea & Barroso, 2022).

Rethink major purchases. You will not only be charged interest when a sizable transaction remains unpaid on your credit record but also lose access to your credit limit. Your credit score will suffer if one or more cards are maxed out until the balances are cleared (Gravier, 2022).

Avoid skipping payments. You'll usually be charged a late payment penalty, which frequently reaches $41. Your interest rate could jump dramatically above your regular purchase APR due to late payments (White, 2023).

Employ a reward-based credit card. Rewards programs present excellent chances to profit from your credit card transactions. With cash-back cards, you receive a percentage of your purchases back. Cards that reward you with points give you at least one point for every dollar you spend. Travel cards typically include travel-related bonuses and privileges, allowing users to accrue travel points (Bareham, 2022).

Failing to understand how credit card payments work can hurt your credit score. Following ten months of planning, Brandon Gomez cleared his $15,000 debt — his most significant balance since using a credit card in 2010. He stopped using credit cards when repaying the debt, resulting in the closure of one of his two accounts. Brandon's debt was paid off by January. After two weeks, the institution handling one of his cards issued him a note saying, *Sorry, we've chosen to suspend your credit card account.*

Since Brandon wanted to avoid accumulating more debt when paying off his loans, he stopped using his card until his balance turned $0. Yet, without warning, his bank canceled his credit line. It declared the account *inactive*, leaving Brandon's credit rating from *excellent* to *bad* overnight.

Creditors use credit scores to assess a debtor's creditworthiness or the probability that they can repay their loan in full and on time.

Your history of borrowing money and repaying it is what creditors in the US normally consider when deciding whether to extend credit to you.

Experian, *TransUnion*, and *Equifax*—three independent credit bureaus—generate the credit reports that describe your credit history

A credit rating ranges from 300 to 850. Creditors use the score to determine your financial risk or whether you can refund your loans on time.

Creditors will analyze your creditworthiness before providing you with credit facilities—timely loan repayments can improve your credit ratings. The upcoming chapter will focus primarily on loans, lenders, and borrowers.

6

UNDERSTANDING LOANS, LENDERS, AND BORROWERS

Nearly 25 million Americans hold at least one personal loan, according to Experian. A Bankrate credit card survey showed that roughly 35% of Americans hold monthly debt (Gillespie, 2023). With high inflation, personal loans are gaining popularity as they could have lower interest rates than credit cards.

Avoiding debt in today's economy is difficult. People are taking on loans to survive due to the high price of necessities and credit card high-interest rates. Learning more about loans can help you eliminate debt and create healthy practices for the future, whether your deficit is decreasing or increasing.

WHAT IS A LOAN?

A loan is a debt that someone (or an entity) incurs. The lender advances the borrower a certain amount of money, often provided by a business, financial institution, or the government. In exchange, the borrower consents to specific terms, including finance charges, interest, a repayment schedule, and other requirements (Kagan, 2021). Sometimes, the lender may demand collateral to protect the loan and guarantee repayment.

You can apply for credit with a bank, business, government, or other entity. The lender may ask you to provide specific information, like your financial background, Social Security Number (SSN), and the loan's purpose. The lender may also review your debt-to-income (DTI) ratio when determining whether you can repay the loan.

The lender may accept or reject your application based on your creditworthiness. Lenders often state the reasons for denying a loan application. If the proposal is accepted, both parties (the lender and the borrower) will sign a contract outlining the terms of the arrangement.

Major purchases, investments, renovations, debt reduction, and company endeavors are just a few uses for loans. Loans can facilitate the expansion of existing businesses. A loan typically has these components:

Principal represents the initial amount someone borrows from a lender.

Loan term is the time frame a borrower must pay back the loan.

Interest rate is the growth rate in the amount owing, commonly called APR (annual percentage rate).

Loan payments mean the amount a debtor pays weekly or monthly to fulfill the terms and conditions of the loan.

REASONS WHY YOU MAY WANT A LOAN AT SOME POINT

It is crucial to consider your financial status before taking out a loan. When you can't afford a significant purchase or project up front, getting a personal loan may be your best option. The most thorough arguments for getting a personal loan are those listed below.

Debt merger. When you request financing to repay multiple obligations, the existing sums are reduced to one monthly fee. Debt consolidation makes it easier to create a plan for repaying your obligations without becoming burdened.

A better option than a cash advance. Utilizing a personal loan rather than a payday loan whenever you need funds for an emergency could result in you paying fewer interest fees. For example, while a payday loan attracts 391% APR, a personal loan typically has an interest rate cap of 36% (Haughn, 2023).

Home renovation. A credit facility can be used by landowners to upgrade their estate or complete appropriate maintenance chores, such as sewage or electrical supply upgrades. Personal loans are typically unsecured; unlike home equity financing, you are not compelled to use your asset as security.

Moving expenses. The average cost of a moving company is $1,250, while a lengthy transfer is $4,890 (Haughn, 2023). If you have insufficient savings to cover the expense of your relocation, you might need to take out a line of credit. Using a personal loan for transportation fees might also assist with staying adrift if you move elsewhere without a career. You won't need to enter your reserves or backup fund this way.

Unexpected costs. A personal loan is usually appropriate for unanticipated medical expenses, especially if your physician expects full payment. After reaching an agreement with the clinic, insurance company, and doctor, you could need a personal loan to cover unanticipated healthcare bills.

Substantial acquisitions. A personal loan can be helpful if you suddenly need to change the transmission in your car, purchase a new washer and dryer, or some other expense but need more money on hand.

Vehicle funding. A personal loan is one option if you aren't purchasing the car straight from the manufacturer. If you buy the automobile from another customer offering their old car, a line of credit will allow you to get it without depleting your funds.

A personal loan might help you meet increased or unexpected expenditures. Yet, it may only sometimes be a perfect idea. Avoid using personal loans when:

- Your credit rating falls into the lowest range. If you need better credit, look for loans for people with less-than-perfect credit, which are available.
- Your monthly loan installments are out of your reach. A personal loan is not practical if your monthly spending is limited.
- You might be eligible for more favorable financing options. If you need a loan for a specific purpose, consider whether a loan created for that purpose will be more advantageous.

Should you prioritize a personal loan over a mortgage? Unlike mortgage loans, personal loans often have five years or fewer maturities. And while personal loans aren't typically used for home purchases, they can be if the lender permits. You may access personal loans of $50,000 or more if you have an excellent credit rating, depending on your qualification and how much the creditor will let you borrow. The range of interest rates is broad, ranging from 3.99% to 36% (Connect, 2018).

Mortgages are loans made expressly for real estate. They are secured by your property, unlike unprotected personal loans. Mortgages come with tax benefits. Real estate taxes, interest, and points are all deductible from your annual taxes. But your house can be foreclosed upon if you cannot make payments.

DIFFERENT TYPES OF LOANS

You can use loans to reach important life goals like going to college or purchasing a home you otherwise couldn't afford. Understanding the kind of loan that will meet your demands is crucial before taking out any loans. The following are the most basic loan types and their main characteristics.

Personal loans. Most personal loans are unsecured, so they don't call for security. They could have a few months to several years of repayment time and variable or fixed interest rates.

Auto loans. When you purchase a car, an auto loan enables you to borrow the purchase price balance, less any down payment. You will use the car as security and may lose it if you don't make payments. Although lengthier loan durations are more prevalent as auto costs rise, the typical auto loan term is between 36 to 72 months (Axelton, 2021).

Student loans. These loans can cover part of graduate and college tuition. Student loans are available from both commercial lenders and the federal government.

Mortgages. The mortgage loan amount equals the home's purchase price, less any down payment. When a mortgage payment is late, the lender may foreclose on the collateral, which is the property. Mortgage payments often take between 10 and 30 years to complete (Axelton, 2021).

Home equity. You can draw up to a particular percentage of the value of your house with a mortgage loan for any reason. Home equities are installment loans—you get a large amount and repay it over time (often between five and thirty years) in consistent monthly installments (Axelton, 2021).

Credit builder. A credit-builder loan may not need a credit check and is intended to help people with bad credit or no credit history rebuild their credit. Usually, between $300 and $1,000, the lender deposits the loan into a savings account. Then, for 6 to 24 months, you make predetermined monthly payments.

You receive the funds back once the loan is paid off (in certain situations, with interest). Before you register for a credit-builder loan, confirm that the creditor reports it to *Experian*, *TransUnion*, and *Equifax* so that on-time payments can boost your credit.

Debt consolidation. You can use a balance transfer loan to pay off high-interest loans, including credit card debt. If the interest rate on these loans is less than the interest rate on your current loans, you can save money.

Payday loans. These short-term loans often have annual percentage rates (APRs) of 400% or higher and require full repayment by your next paycheck (Axelton, 2021). These loans, which you can obtain from physical or online payday lenders, often have amounts ranging from $50 to $1,000 and don't involve a credit check. Avoid using these loans because they are predatory—for example since repaying payday loans is challenging, employees renew them, incurring extra charges and falling deeper into debt.

INTEREST AND PRINCIPAL

When you borrow money up to a particular level, you are responsible for more than that sum. In return for providing the funds, financial institutions charge a fee known as interest (Gogol, 2022). Comprehending the distinction between repaying a loan's principal and interest is critical.

Interest is a cost for borrowing money calculated using the APR, a proportion of loan principal. The portion of each transaction that applies to interest is the interest payment for a loan. Usually, interest payments are made in installments.

The principal balance is the sum of the loaned funds that the debtor still owes, interest-free. The portion of each payment designated for the principal balance is the primary payment.

Is it wiser to make payments on the interest or the principal first? Generally, you want to make principal payments as frequently as possible. You spend more money when you pay interest on a loan. Keeping track of your debts requires understanding what percentage of your expenses are allocated to interest. You need to determine your APR and principal balance.

Multiply the principal balance by the APR and divide the result by 12 to calculate your monthly interest payments. For example, if the APR of your $10,000 loan is 6%, your monthly interest payment is $50. The principal balance would remain unchanged if you paid precisely $50 monthly.

Principal repayment. Every time you pay, the amount over the interest payment reduces the principal. So, the quicker the principal balance decreases and the less interest you must pay, the more you pay off monthly. Using the example above, if you spend $100 monthly, your principal balance gets reduced by $50 monthly.

Have you got a lot of debt to pay off? Examine refinancing. Many people are caught in a cycle where they only pay interest on their debts, leaving the principal unpaid. Borrowers can break this cycle by refinancing. When a borrower refinances, all their debts are consolidated under one lender, with one rate and one monthly payment. Refinancing frequently results in the borrower receiving reduced interest rates and simplifies repayment (Gogol, 2022).

INTEREST RATES EXPLAINED

The interest rate is the fee a lender levies on a borrower, expressed as a percentage of the principal.

Also subject to interest rates CD (certificate of deposit) and savings account earnings. Annual percentage yield (APY) is the interest earned on these bank accounts (Banton, 2023).

Since lenders expect compensation for the money's diminished value during the loan period, the amount due is generally more than the amount borrowed. Instead of giving a loan during that time, the lender may have invested the money, which would have resulted in asset-producing income. The interest charged distinguishes between the total amount repaid and the principal borrowed.

Simple interest. Suppose an annual loan agreement for $300,000 specifies a 4% simple interest rate. You will pay $312,000 at the end of the loan term. If it were simply a one-year lending agreement, you would be required to pay $12,000 in interest.

Compound interest. Both the principal and the interest accrued over time are subject to compound interest. The creditor assumes that the borrower will still owe the principal amount plus interest after the first year. The creditor further believes that the borrower will be in debt for the principal amount and interest on the interest from the first year after the second year.

Compound interest is advantageous when accumulating money in a savings account. Compound interest is paid on these accounts as payment to account holders for permitting the bank to use their deposits.

Although interest rates are a source of income for the lender, they are a cost of borrowing for the borrower. Businesses compare the cost of borrowing versus the cost of equity, including dividend payments, when evaluating which funding source will be the least expensive. The price of the capital is assessed to create the ideal capital structure because most businesses finance their capital through equity issuance.

APR (annual percentage rate) vs. APY (annual percentage yield). Consumer loan interest rates are often stated as APR. For the opportunity to borrow their money, lenders require a specific rate of return. What you earn on your savings or CD account is APY (Banton, 2023).

A nation's central bank determines the interest rate, and each bank bases its APR range on that rate. The price of debt increases when the central bank establishes interest rates at a top standard. High-interest rates deter borrowers and impede consumer demand. Moreover, interest rates typically increase along with inflation.

The actual rate of interest, commonly referred to as the APR, is what a bank uses when it provides you with an interest rate quote. Banks may also tie your interest rate to a particular benchmark. If such a clause is present in your loan, changes in this benchmark will affect how much you will pay in interest (Carlson, 2022).

Suppose you took a one-year $1,000 loan from a bank and paid $1,060 at the end of the loan term. Divide the interest ($60) by the principal ($1,000) to know the interest rate.

While the average APR for personal loans in 2019 was 9.41%, a 24-month personal loan attracted a 9.34% APR in the third quarter of 2020 (George, 2023). Yet, because your credit history affects the rate you qualify for, you may be authorized for loans with interest rates below or above the industry standard.

The interest rates you are offered will depend on your circumstances when requesting a loan, the specifics of the loan you are looking for, and the creditor you have selected. Your loan rate may be impacted by many important factors, including:

Credit rating. Higher credit scores allow borrowers to receive loans at more favorable terms.

Earnings and livelihood. You'll need to show evidence of a dependable job and a considerable salary to persuade a lender that you can repay the money you are looking to borrow.

Fixed or variable. Your monthly payment and interest rate will never change with a fixed-rate loan. Unlike fixed rates, variable rates fluctuate over time. Variable-rate personal loans typically have lower starting interest rates than fixed-rate loans. The cost of borrowing on a varying loan may look cheaper initially, but it may rise with time (George, 2023).

Secured or unsecured. When requesting a secured loan, you pledge an asset, like your house or vehicle, as security. Most personal loans are unsecured; therefore, you are not required to provide protection.

Payback schedule. Interest rates would be higher if you took out a loan for a longer duration because the lender would be taking on more risk. The interest rate for a loan with a quick payback time frame ought to be lower than that of a loan with a more extended repayment date.

Large principal loans. Larger loans might occasionally pose a greater risk to creditors, so rates may be higher.

LENDERS AND BORROWERS

Lenders are corporations or financial institutions that give credit to people and businesses. The interest the lender earns is a percentage of the borrower's loan. If you have taken credit, you are the borrower and you may pay the debt in installments, such as monthly payments or a lump sum later (CFI, 2023).

Lenders and borrowers both have the option of starting the lending procedure. Most frequently, the borrower applies for a loan at the bank and must fill out an application. The application must contain the desired loan amount, the planned usage, current cash flows or earnings, the borrower's physical address, and the addresses and names of any guarantors, among other details.

A proposal to give credit to a person or a business on specific terms may also come from the bank. In such a situation, the potential borrowers are frequently high-net-worth people and high-growth companies who may often require financing for investment or working capital finance. There are two major categories of lenders—direct and secondary market lenders.

Direct. A direct lender gives the borrower a loan without any intermediaries. Direct lenders frequently include banks and credit unions and are generally associated with mortgage loans. It's also crucial to remember that mortgage brokers and direct lenders essentially offer the same loan terms and prices. But, since a broker will also receive a portion of the deal, you could have to spend a little more on their services (FindLaw, 2023).

Secondary market. FNMA (Federal National Mortgage Association) is a typical example of this lender. Many small-scale lenders get their money from secondary market lenders. These auxiliary financial institutions have helped the national mortgage market by facilitating simple interstate money transfers. Mortgages are not restricted to a few regions thanks to the flow of loan funds. Also, the secondary creditors have set out rules and laws that benefit the general population.

An applicant for money is a borrower. They are also known as the party that owes the debt or the debtor. Per the terms and conditions set forth by the two parties, interest is payable on the loan. *Borrower* describes a person or legal entity that accepts a financial loan, item, or service on credit from a commercial lender. Borrowers get money in exchange for a required guarantee, depending on their credit score, a specified duration, and payback terms (WSM, n.d.). To combat inflation and its rise, borrowers facilitate money movement throughout the economy.

Large-scale industrial or corporate endeavors, such as mining, require enormous cash, which can only be obtained via borrowing from lending organizations. While creditors generate income from interest collected on debtor's accounts, borrowers are the foundation of banks.

Borrower's Rights

- The loan agreement has to meet the debtor's requirements.
- The documentation and the loan agreement must be provided to the debtor in tangible copies by the lender.
- Monthly loan statements that include the intermediaries' documentation of payment history are provided to the debtor.
- The debtor must be given access to the credit score by the lender.
- Lenders cannot accept any terms or fees not disclosed in the loan agreement.

Borrower's Obligations

- Provide permission for the lender to obtain your credit score from credit rating organizations and pay any associated fees.

- All financial and personal information documentation must be genuine and free from forgery.
- The debtor must uphold the loan arrangement.
- They are required to make the installment payments by the deadline.
- They need to make a payment on the debt.
- The debtor must use the amount of the loan that the bank approved.

HOW TO COMPARE LOAN CONDITIONS

Suppose you work for a large corporation and are trying to get a property loan. You are currently unsure of which bank to get the funding from even when you have two available choices—*ABHC* bank is ready to offer you an 18-year term loan with 8.5% APR. *KCKC* bank wants a 20-year term loan with 8.25% APR but would levy you a 0.50% service fee, usually talked about in "points". You must pay the service fee in advance. Both banks offer the monthly installment payment option. If you want to borrow $150,000, which banks would you choose?

Getting the best and least expensive loan can be challenging if you have many loan options. Finding the most outstanding deal might take a lot of work due to the variety of loan conditions, deadlines, and monthly installments. Before selecting the ideal loan for you, there are a few fundamental factors to consider and evaluate.

Loan term. Evaluate the various loan terms and go with the shortest duration. While a shorter loan period will probably result in higher monthly payments, you will spend less on interest altogether (Campbell, 2018). Consider taking out a longer-term loan if, for some circumstances, the shorter loan period carries a higher percentage rate. If there is no prepayment penalty, consider making more significant installments.

APR. Unlike interest rates reflecting the primary interest charged, APR also considers costs like points and origination fees. For mortgages, creditors are mandated to provide you with the APR; analyzing the APRs is preferable to identify which loan would cost you more over time.

Lump sum. These loans typically contain a balloon payment that must be made to cover the principal balance owing after the loan period. Remember that you'll have that cash on hand to meet the lump sum deposit when due, or you will need to refinance.

Total expenses. If you can handle the monthly payments, select the loan with the lowest total amount due over the duration.

Monthly payment. Consider your financial situation again if you have a loan with a low monthly fee or an interest-only payment pushing you beyond your means. Choose the loan with the shortest duration and lowest interest rate generally, as long as you manage the monthly payment.

> You can apply for credit with a bank, business, government, or other entity. The lender may ask you to provide specific information, like your financial background, Social Security Number, and the loan's purpose. The lender may also review your debt-to-income (DTI) ratio when determining whether you can repay the loan.
>
> You can use loans to reach important life goals like going to college or purchasing a home you otherwise couldn't afford. Understanding the kind of loan that will meet your demands is crucial before taking out any loans. The following are the most basic loan types and their main characteristics.
>
> When you borrow money up to a particular level, you are responsible for more than that sum. In return for providing the funds, financial institutions charge a fee known as interest.

Understanding loan management can help you achieve your primary life goals. Whether you're paying for school, buying a home, or meeting other financial goals, knowing the right loan for your needs is critical. The next chapter discusses how to eliminate and avoid getting into debt.

7

AVOIDING AND ELIMINATING DEBT

Consumers added more than $1 trillion to their total debt in 2022, a remarkable growth not seen in more than ten years. High inflation levels and substantial consumer demand increases prohibited already cash-flush consumers from cutting back on their spending. The Federal Reserve's escalation of interest rates is a factor that will almost certainly influence consumer borrowing habits in 2023.

Mortgage affordability and home prices have changed, variable-rate credit card interest rates have steadily increased and currently average close to 20%, and personal loan activity has significantly increased. Below 25% of American homes are debt-free, based on Experian research. This amount could be low for various reasons, including the large proportion of auto loans and home mortgages that many people have (Horymski, 2023).

More and more people are going into debt. In cases like student loans, this can be considered an investment in their future. However, in subjects like consumer debt, avoid those unfortunate circumstances.

WHAT IS DEBT?

A debt is anything that one party owes another party, typically money. Many people and businesses use debt to finance major purchases they sometimes cannot afford. A debt must be repaid, frequently with additional interest, unless the lender overlooks it. Loans, such as mortgages, vehicle loans, personal loans, and credit cards, are the most prevalent debt (Chen, 2023).

Most loans have a set repayment amount due by a specific date, which could be years or months. The borrower is typically given a certain amount of money in the loan agreement, and the loan's conditions will specify the sum of interest the borrower must pay or a percentage of the loan sum. The lender receives interest as payment for the loan's inherent risk.

There are some differences between how lines of credit and credit cards work. With no predetermined end date, they offer so-called revolving or open-end credit.

The borrower gets a credit limit, and as long as they don't exceed the limit, they can use their credit line or credit card regularly.

Good vs. Bad Debt

A company's debt is a significant concern in corporate finance. A corporation might be unable to pay back its loans if sales decline for whatever reason and it is no longer as valuable as it previously was. Such a business runs the danger of failing. A company that does not borrow money could be limiting its ability to grow (CFI, 2023).

Every industry on the market has a unique relationship with debt. As a result, each business determines the appropriate level of debt, using scales specific to its sector. When analyzing a company's financials, people consider many variables to determine if its debt level is within acceptable bounds.

Good debt enables a person or business to manage their finances properly, making it simple to grow their current wealth. They may buy what they need and be well-prepared for unforeseen circumstances. Things that fall under this category include mortgages, purchasing products and services that save the consumer money, student loans, and debt reduction.

A bad debt is an obligation whose value drops immediately after purchase. However, most necessities in life, like vehicles and clothing, meet that criterion. Payday loans and credit card loans are more instances.

DIFFERENT TYPES OF DEBT

The simplest definition of debt is when someone borrows money and promises to repay it. Student loans, mortgages, and credit card transactions are typical examples. However, did you know there are various sorts of debt, not just those loans? Making financial decisions can be aided by a knowledge of debt classifications and how they operate.

Secured debt. A secured debt decreases the creditor's risks because an asset (collateral) backs secured debt. The collateral thus secures the loan. Cash or property can be collateral, but the debtor may forfeit the collateral if they don't pay on time (Capital One, 2021).

Remember that there may be further repercussions if you don't pay a secured loan. For example, creditors may submit debtors' late payments to credit reporting agencies. A protected credit card needs a money deposit before being used for transactions.

Secured debt also includes mortgages and auto loans. In those situations, the purchased item—such as the apartment or the car—typically serves as collateral. Collateral can have a silver lining—less risk for the lender may translate into better conditions and rates for the borrower. Some lenders might also be less picky about the required credit ratings.

Unsecured debt. When a debt is unprotected, there is no requirement for collateral. Think of personal loans, credit cards, or student loans. There are some exemptions for various types of student loans. Still, without security, your credit will play a significant role in deciding if you qualify for unprotected debt. Simply because a loan is unsecured, missing payments are not necessarily acceptable. Late payments may still affect your credit, resulting in collections or legal action.

Revolving debt. Revolving debt may be something you are already familiar with if you have an unprotected or protected credit card. As long as the account is in good shape, you can charge money into and pay off debt using a running credit account indefinitely. Revolving credit includes personal credit lines and home equity lines of credit.

Your lender will establish a credit limit if they approve you for this credit line. The amount you use each month determines how much credit you have available. The minimum payment amounts may also vary each month and interest is added to any balance carried over to the following billing cycle.

Installment debt. There are many ways in which installment debt is different from revolving debt. It is closed-ended, as opposed to revolving credit. It shows that it is paid back over a set time. Payments are sometimes made in equal monthly increments, hence the name. Mortgages and auto loans fall under this category. When you pay off installment debt, you pay the interest and principal simultaneously (Capital One, 2021).

HOW TO PREVENT YOURSELF FROM BUILDING UP BAD DEBT

To prevent debt, you must have a sound financial approach and avoid frivolous goals that bring relatively brief delight but generate long-term strain on your bank statement. These tactics can help prevent debt (Central Bank, n.d.).

Avoid purchasing something you couldn't afford with cash. Living under the false impression that you can pay for things you cannot afford is one of the riskiest ways to use a credit card. If you can't get something with cash, don't purchase it with a card.

Keep emergency money on hand. Save up at least six months' worth of your pay when attempting to build an emergency fund. This will be enough to meet your unanticipated expenses.

Clear credit card debt. Paying off your credit card amount in little increments is the best strategy for controlling your expenditures. To avoid life getting in the way, make your payment the following day if you use your credit card to make a purchase.

Prioritize needs over wants. There is usually room in your budget to eliminate wasteful spending patterns. Limit your internet purchasing and eating out. Your financial situation will improve as you spend just on necessities and cut less on wants.

Make a budget. Determine how much money to put into your 401(k) savings and how much more you have each month to spend on needs.

Only carry a few cards. The more charges you have on each card, the easier it will be to forget about purchases and payments.

Track expenses. Record your expenditures you can update monthly. If you have several accounts and credit cards, pay off each one in full and on time. If you get a pay raise, live off the nominal wages you previously received and save the additional money. Put the extra money where it will work harder for you.

HOW TO ELIMINATE DEBT

When paying off debt is a goal, there are various things you may do to accomplish it in a year or less, or at the very least, to pay off most of it. Adopting these financial strategies may help you get out of debt.

Use a budget. Track your earnings and expenses. By becoming more aware of your income and costs, you may eliminate or reduce frivolous spending (Westchester County, n.d.).

Avoid accruing extra debt. Before taking on any additional debt, work toward paying off what you already owe. Buy what is necessary. It will be harder to manage your debt if you accumulate more debt by purchasing frivolous expenditures while you still owe money.

Clear your debts. You may avoid paying outrageous interest rates and overdue charges by making up-to-date repayments on your bills. If you cannot complete the total costs, try to pay above the minimum amount required to reduce the interest and fees you incur.

Examine your bills. After you receive your receipts and reports, double-check the correctness and reliability of your tariffs. If errors occur or your payments unexpectedly increase, notify your creditor immediately.

Repay high-interest deficits first. If you have several financial obligations to pay off, settling those with the highest interest will lead to a lesser total sum (Westchester County, n.d.).

Search for the lowest interest rates when combining your liabilities. By acquiring a debt reduction loan from a credit union or bank, you can manage your bills more effectively because you have to make a single payment to the credit union or bank rather than many transactions to all of your present lenders. Before consolidating, check around for the most effective rate because the credit union or bank often gives you an interest rate higher than the rates on the debts you owe.

Discuss repayment strategies with your lenders. Talk with the companies to which you owe money. They may consent to lower repayments and devise a payment arrangement that is more acceptable for their financial circumstances.

Consult credit advisors. Consider talking to a credit counselor if you need assistance in creating a plan for repaying your debt. Counselors that promise to pay off all of your debt effortlessly for a small charge should be avoided since they can operate under pretenses.

Bob and Suzie had difficulty meeting their monthly installments and faced financial pressure threatening their health. They were out of cash and couldn't cater for necessities like utilities and food. Diminished household income, limited budget, using credit to purchase household items, and vehicle upgrades, including several everyday life events, racked up loads of debts for the family.

After submitting a refinance application at their bank, Bob and Suzie couldn't get approval because their current deficit was too much for their income level. They thought they would need to sell their property or file for bankruptcy to clear their high-interest debts; they didn't know there were debt relief options to salvage their situation.

They consulted financial experts, encouraging them to review their choices and balance their budgets. They combined their deficits into one monthly payment, and they negotiated a lower interest rate with their creditors. As their stress levels decreased, they tracked their expenses, modified their budget, and worked towards other financial objectives. Bob and Suzie accessed free online money management tools and classes to ensure they acquired the knowledge to clear their debts and prevent relying on credit for future purchases. After a year of living without credit, they became debt-free.

> A debt is anything that one party owes another party, typically money. Many people and businesses use debt to finance major purchases they sometimes cannot afford.
>
> Secured debt also includes mortgages and auto loans. In those situations, the purchased item—such as the apartment or the car—typically serves as collateral. Collateral can have a silver lining—less risk for the lender may translate into better conditions and rates for the borrower. Some lenders might also be less picky about the required credit ratings.
>
> To prevent debt, you must have a sound financial approach and avoid frivolous goals that bring relatively brief delight but generate long-term strain on your bank statement.
>
> Consider talking to a credit counselor if you need assistance creating a plan for repaying your debt. Counselors that promise to pay off all of your debt effortlessly for a small charge should be avoided since they can operate under pretenses.

Developing sound financial techniques and avoiding frivolous objectives or payments are vital tricks for managing or eliminating your debts. The next chapter will educate you about the importance of preparing for retirement by harnessing workplace retirement plans.

8

PREPARING FOR LATER: WORKPLACE RETIREMENT PLANS

When should I begin making retirement savings?

The reply is straightforward: *as early as you can*. The optimal moment for saving is in your twenties, shortly after you graduate from college and begin working (CNN Money, n.d.). Suppose you started retirement savings at 25 and contributed $3,000 yearly for ten years. If your investment account had a 7% annual return, your $30,000 investment will be over $338,000 by age 65.

Retirement plans help create an additional layer for your retirement funds, frequently financially supported by employers. While only some employers offer these types of help, it is essential to ask and figure out what your options are.

EMPLOYER-SPONSORED RETIREMENT PLANS

401(k)

Payments to a 401(k) scheme by employees are tax deductible. Automatic donations are taken from employees' paychecks and put into their chosen funds. The accounts have a $22,500 yearly contribution cap in 2023 and $30,000 for individuals over 50 (Yochim, 2023).

Traditional or standard 401(k) deducts contributions from your wages before the IRS takes its portion, allowing your money to grow tax free. Pre-tax payments to a 401(k) can increase your ability to save and reduce your annual taxable income.

Assuming you earn $65,000 annually and contribute $19,500 to your 401(k). You will only be responsible for paying income taxes on $45,500 of your compensation rather than the $65,000 you earned. Putting money aside for the future allows you to avoid paying taxes on $19,500.

Roth 401(k). If your workplace provides a Roth 401(k), you can make after-tax contributions, and when you retire, your payouts will be tax free. Since your payments were made with after-tax money, you have already paid your dues. In addition, the account's earnings—including interest and stock dividends—are tax free.

The yearly limit on contributions to your 401(k) plans has grown due to rising inflation. Individuals could make a $20,500 contribution in 2022. By 2023, it had increased to $22,500. The new cap is $30,000 in 2023 instead of $27,000 in 2022 for those 50 or older (Yochim, 2023). Your company will make a specified financial commitment based on your 401(k) contribution. An employer may provide a partial or complete match. While a partial match implies that your boss will add a fraction of your 401(k) contribution, your company may contribute the same amount as you do in a whole matching arrangement.

How much employer contributions you own depends on how long you've worked for the company; this is known as vesting. The average vesting term for 401(k) contributions is five years (Piburn, 2022). So, if you quit your job or get fired before the vesting time has passed, you may lose the employer match.

Embracing 401(k) contributions lowers your taxable earnings. Suppose your taxable income is $31,000 if you file as a single person. The figure becomes $29,000 after contributing $2,000 to your 401(k) account. Matching-contribution clauses are a common feature of corporate plans offered by employers. The advantages provided by your employer are forfeited if you don't participate and don't make salary-deferral contributions (Appleby, 2023).

Pooled Employer Plans

A *pooled employer strategy* is a multi-employer plan created to relieve businesses of various administrative responsibilities. This lessens the organizational complexity of the program and lowers liability, making it more appealing to smaller employers. Suppose you have considered offering a retirement plan but have yet to do so. In that case, a pooled employer plan is a fantastic alternative.

It also makes logical sense if you already have a plan but want to minimize your involvement in managing it. As a professionally managed retirement plan, it offers companies a streamlined administration process, decreased liability, and the opportunity for cost savings from resource sharing (Paychex, 2023). These are enormous benefits of using pooled employer plans (PEP):

Saving businesses money on overhead fees. Employers may save administrative expenses and realize economies of scale by combining assets into one sizable plan.

Reduced fiduciary risk. The pooled plan provider takes on most fiduciary duties. Select a provider that upholds industry norms, follows deadlines, and performs general obligations to ensure the plan runs smoothly.

Enhanced technical expertise. Many companies lack the resources—infrastructure, technology, and time—to perform the tasks involved in retirement administration. PEPs relieve employers of the burden of managing the many 401(k) intricacies, including setup, form filing, and employee registration.

Potential for tax credits. The SECURE Act stipulates that qualified employers may be entitled to obtain tax credits totaling up to $5,000 per year to help defray initial costs. For the first three years, they can also take advantage of a $500 extra tax credit offered for employing automatic enrollment in the program (Paychex, 2023).

What differentiates a PEP from 401(k) plans? A 401(k) generally gives you greater authority, but managing one might be more complex and involve more effort as the employer. In contrast, you would have less influence over a PEP (but less financial and legal responsibility).

SIMPLE IRA

Employer-sponsored SIMPLE IRA is designed especially for small enterprises with 100 workers or fewer.

If your employees earned $5,000 or more in the previous two years and anticipate earning that amount this year, they can enroll in the plan. You can set aside some of your employees' salaries for retirement using a SIMPLE IRA. The funds will increase tax free until they are withdrawn at retirement. More than $13,500 cannot be deposited into this category of an account by you or your workers in 2020 (The Hartford, n.d.).

Pros

- **Few forms to fill out**. If any documentation is required, it is typically less than what is needed to set up a 401(k).
- **Minimal setup and upkeep prices**. Some retirement plans impose steep account opening and maintenance fees. Your company often incurs fewer up-front and operating expenses with SIMPLE IRAs.
- **Tax deductible investments**. Contributions by employers and employees are deductible on tax returns.

Cons

- **Employer-matching prerequisite**. The IRS mandates that companies match employee

contributions up to a predetermined amount, dollar for dollar.
- **Withdrawal requisites.** Up to the age of 59½, you cannot take funds from your SEP IRA. If you remove funds before that time, you will pay a 10% penalty.
- **Absence of a Roth version.** You cannot deposit after-tax funds into your account.

IRS-approved sample plans are typically available through banks and other financial organizations. Following the initial setup of your SIMPLE IRAs, you and your staff can set up recurring payroll deductions for pre-tax contributions.

SEP Plans

A simplified employee pension plan (SEP) enables employers to contribute towards retirement. The company makes discretionary contributions to each eligible employee's plan, and employer payments to a SEP IRA are tax deductible (Fresh Books, 2023).

A SEP IRA has few start-ups and ongoing expenses that conventional employer-sponsored retirement plans incur. An employer must establish a SEP IRA by signing a written agreement outlining the plan's advantages, informing their employees of the arrangement, and opening an IRA for each participant employee.

The maximum acceptable compensation contribution is $330,000 in 2023, regardless of income. The figure was $290,000 in 2021. Participants may borrow up to $50,000, but at most 50% of their vested amount, under the SEP. The SEP plan is only open to employees at least 21 years old. They should have earned at least $650 from their employer in 2022 and have worked in the company for at least three of the previous five years (Fresh Books, 2023).

Pros

- You can optimize savings by limiting contributions.
- By making deductible contributions, you can lower your tax obligation.
- It enables you to plan for your financial future and aids workers in getting ready for retirement.
- The tax payments on the donation might be postponed until retirement age.

Cons

- Employees cannot make direct contributions.
- Employees are totally dependent on their employers to put aside their contributions.

Profit-Sharing Plans (PSPs)

This program enables businesses to support employee retirement savings. Employers use these programs to give their employees a stake in the company's success. It's a fantastic perk that attracts new employees (Phipps, 2022).

Profit-sharing payments to employees could be in stock or cash. After the age of 59½, these accounts permit withdrawals without incurring penalties. Some programs provide both cash and deferred benefits. Ordinary income tax rates apply to the money.

One distinction between PSP and 401(k) is whether the employer matches the employee's savings efforts at a predetermined rate or corporate profitability. While 401(k) plans are supported mainly by the employee's earnings, profit-sharing techniques are entirely covered by the company.

Although there is a cap on the sum that can be made for each employee, there is no set amount that a firm must contribute to its profit-sharing plan every year. A profit-sharing plan's maximum contribution was 25% of pay, or $61,000 in 2022. The figure was $58,000 in 2021. Additionally, there are restrictions on how much of your payment is used to calculate contributions—

while the max is $305,000 for the tax year 2022, the amount was $290,000 in 2021 (Phipps, 2022).

Employee Stock Ownership Plans (ESOPs)

This program gives a company's workers ownership stakes. Each eligible employee receives a predetermined percentage of the company's stock shares with no upfront costs from the business. Until an employee leaves the company or retires, the assets for an employee stock ownership plan are kept in a trust unit for security and growth. Following their departure, the corporation repurchases the shares and distributes them to more employees (CFI, 2022).

When a business wishes to establish an ESOP, it must set up a trust to deposit new company stock shares or money to purchase existing stock. To the extent allowed by law, these trust donations are tax deductible. Following that, the stakes are distributed across each employee's individual accounts. The allocation calculation often includes remuneration, years of service, or a combination.

New workers must frequently work for the program for at least a year before enrolling and earning payments. Before employees are eligible to receive the shares they were allotted through an ESOP, the shares must vest. In this context, vesting refers to employees' rising rights on their claims as they gain organizational seniority.

Pros

- **Tax advantages for workers**. The contributions made to an ESOP are tax free for the employees. Only after retirement or when an employee leaves the company are they subject to taxation.
- **More engaged employees**. Employees can access the company's long-term goals and suggest the business's direction. An ESOP also improves employee confidence in the industry.
- **Favorable business results**. One recent Rutgers University study found that adopting ESOP enhanced job growth and business performance (CFI, 2022).

Cons

- **Inadequate diversity**. The workers commit their savings to the same business that provides them with perks like insurance and wages. Employees run the danger of losing money if the firm fails.

- **Restricts recent hires.** Opportunities for newer employees to participate in essential choices are limited.

457 Plans

State and local public companies, as well as some nonprofit organizations, provide 457 plans, which are retirement savings plans with tax advantages. The Internal Revenue Code (IRC) section 457(b) is the foundation of 457 retirement plans. It was established on November 6, 1978, with the enactment of the Revenue Act. It first only applied to employers in state and local governments (Jones, n.d.).

Government 457. They may be provided by state, municipal, and public schools. Usually, all staff who meet the plan's qualification requirements are eligible to enroll.

Top hat. Only a few managers or highly compensated staff can access them; tax-exempt entities like nonprofit hospitals and charities often make them available.

You can deduct contributions up to 100% of your accessible income or the yearly contribution cap to a government 457 plan. The maximum annual contribution for 2022 is $20,500 (Jones, n.d.).

The details of your plan will determine whether you can make Roth contributions to your 457 programs. Taxes on your payment and earnings are postponed with pre-tax contributions until you receive a dividend from the plan. No tax break for people making a Roth contribution because they are paying with after-tax money.

Government 457 Withdrawal Rules

Typically, you are only permitted to withdraw funds from a Governmental 457(b) plan when a particular triggering event takes place, such as:

- Separation from the military (employment).
- Reaching the age of 70½.
- Termination of the program (all participants and workers become 100% vested).

You must start implementing a required minimum distribution (RMD) from your strategy by April 1 of the year after you reach 72 and by December 31 of each succeeding year.

403(b) Plans

People who operate in public education and those employed by tax-exempt organizations may open a 403(b) plan as a retirement account. It resembles the better-known 401(k) version, which managers in the private sector more frequently provide.

A 403(b) allows for yearly contributions of $20,500 and $22,500 in 2022 and 2023, respectively. The maximum annual contribution for people aged 50 and older is $30,000 ($27,000 in 2022). Your company may decide to match a percentage of your contributions to a 403(b) account, which allows you to set aside a part of each paycheck for retirement (Hagen, 2023).

Pros

- **Tax benefits.** You may benefit from a lower tax payment this year in exchange for taxes on withdrawals in retirement if you choose a regular or a Roth 403(b). If you pay taxes on your donations, you may also benefit from tax-free withdrawals in retirement.
- **Company matching.** Employers offering 403(b) plans may pledge to match a portion of their staff's personal contributions.
- **Reduced vesting periods.** When your employer-matched money becomes yours depends on the vesting schedules. The length of the 403(b) vesting schedules differs from business to company. It is often shorter than the 401(k) vesting schedules.

Cons

- **Limited investing options.** Compared to a 401(k), this type of account provides more constrained investing alternatives.
- **High premiums.** Some 403(b)s have higher costs that can reduce your profits, but not all of them.
- **Early withdrawal charges.** You'll incur a 10% early withdrawal penalty if you take money from your tax-deferred 403(b) before turning 59½. The fine is waived if you have an acceptable excuse, such as a substantial medical bill (Hagen, 2023).

Cash-Balance Plans

A cash balance plan expresses the promised reward as a specified account balance. An annual "pay credit" is added to a participant's account under a typical cash balance plan (such as 5 percent of compensation from their employer). The participant gets an interest credit at a variable or fixed rate (USDL, 2011).

The benefit amounts offered to participants are not immediately affected by changes in the value of the plan's investments. Therefore, the employer is the only party who bears the investment risks. Members can roll that payout into an IRA when they receive a lump sum payment.

What Distinguishes Cash Balance Programs From 401(K)s?

Participation. Employees who engage in cash balance programs are only sometimes required to donate a percentage of their wages to the scheme. The employee's decision to contribute to the plan determines whether they can participate in a 401(k).

Financial risks. The employer (or an investment manager they have hired) manages the investments for cash balance plans and takes on investment risks. Members in 401(k) plans are frequently allowed to choose their assets within specific categories. Participants in 401(k) plan take on the risks and benefits of their chosen investments.

Non-Qualified Deferred Compensations (NQDCs)

Deferred compensation plans are basically contracts between you and your company that state that you will be paid later. Deferred compensation plans come in two varieties: qualified and non-qualified deferred compensations. The two types of plans differ in how the law uses and interprets them (Stinnett, 2023).

NQDCs vs. Qualified Deferred Plans

Qualified deferred compensation schemes must follow Employee Retirement Income Security Act regulations. (ERISA). Rules determine NQDC plans; however, these regulations aren't as rigorous for these programs.

Eligible deferred compensation plans have financial constraints, which is another significant distinction between the two types of projects. A 401(k) is a suitable deferred compensation plan. There is a cap on the amount you can donate each tax year. Since NQDC plans do not have contribution limits, they can therefore be helpful to high-earners who desire to contribute more than is permitted by qualified deferred compensation plans.

Only some people should participate in non-qualified deferred compensation programs. Considering whether participating in one makes sense and is wise, given your financial situation. For instance, if you're not maxing out your 401(k) each year, enrolling in an NQDC plan to increase your retirement savings may be worthless.

VARIETIES OF NON-EMPLOYER-SPONSORED RETIREMENT PROGRAMS

Traditional Individual Retirement Accounts (IRAs)

People can put pre-tax income in investments that grow tax-deferred using the traditional IRA. According to the IRS, beneficiaries are subject to capital gains or dividend income taxes once they remove funds. Traditional IRAs are held by custodians, which include commercial banks and retail brokers. The invested funds are distributed among various investment vehicles per the instructions of the account holder and per the available options.

According to the account holder's age, the IRS imposes annual limits on contributions to a traditional IRA. For savers under 50, the maximum contribution is $6000 for the tax year 2022 and $6500 for the following year. Following a catch-up contribution option, those aged 50 and older have more significant yearly contribution limits that allow an extra $1,000. The IRS considers distributions from regular IRA's ordinary income and taxes them accordingly. The earliest age at which account holders may receive dividends is 59½ (Hayes, 2023).

Suppose you or your spouse received taxable income the year you wish to contribute and intend to file a joint tax return. In that case, you are eligible to start a traditional IRA. You can open a regular IRA if you and your partner are employed. Setting up a conventional personal IRA can be helped by several businesses, financial institutions, or brokerage houses. IRS code requirements must be followed, and your account's custodian will handle those responsibilities on your behalf.

Roth IRAs

In a Roth IRA, you can make after-tax contributions to a specific kind of tax-advantaged individual retirement account. All subsequent withdrawals from a Roth IRA are tax free after the initial grant, which is taxed. Both regular and Roth IRAs are subject to the same contribution caps. Even if you have various accounts, you can only donate up to the maximum since these limits apply to all your IRAs (Segal, 2023). A Roth IRA offers investment choices, including mutual funds, equities, bonds, and bitcoin.

Use an organization granted IRS authorization (such as brokerages, credit unions, or banks) to sell IRAs to establish a Roth IRA. The holder must provide two crucial records when setting an IRA:

- IRA reporting form
- IRA acceptance deal and roadmap letter

These records describe the rules and guidelines the Roth IRA must comply with and serve as a treaty between the IRA holder and the curator or manager.

Do Roth IRAs have insurance? If a bank maintains your funds, you should know that IRAs are covered by a different type of insurance than regular deposit accounts. Although account balances are aggregated rather than seen individually, the Federal Deposit Insurance Corp. (FDIC) provides insurance coverage for traditional or Roth IRA accounts up to $250,000 (Segal, 2023).

Roth IRAs only accept earned income as a contribution. Commissions, salaries, wages, bonuses, and other sums paid to employees for services rendered are all considered remuneration for funding a Roth IRA. Anyone can participate if they comply with a specific filing status and adjusted gross income standards.

One method couples might raise their investments is through a spousal Roth IRA. A spouse who earns a meager income can have their Roth IRA funded by their partner. The regulations and restrictions to regular Roth IRA contributions also apply to spouse-related Roth IRA contributions. Because Roth IRAs cannot be joint accounts, the spouse's Roth IRA is kept apart from the contributor's Roth IRA (Segal, 2023).

You can withdraw Roth IRA contributions anytime during the tax year without incurring any taxes or penalties.

Roth vs. Traditional IRAs

The filer's taxable income will determine if a Roth IRA is better than a standard IRA, including their anticipated retirement tax rates and personal preferences. The Roth IRA may be more favorable for persons anticipating higher tax brackets when they retire since the total amount of taxes they will not pay in retirement will be more than the income taxes they will pay now. A Roth IRA is most advantageous for younger and lower-income employees.

Payroll Deduction IRAs

Payroll deduction IRAs offer a mechanism to motivate employees to save for the future. It is a simple way for workers who aren't protected by employer-sponsored retirement plans to make saving for retirement (Tretina & Schmidt, 2022).

Pros

- **Reduced fees**. No regulatory, administrative, or other expenses are associated with setting up and managing this retirement plan.

- **No federal filings are necessary**. While using payroll deduction IRAs, you don't have to file any documentation with the government or IRS or provide a yearly report.

Cons

- **Minimal savings**. The contribution limit for payroll deduction IRAs is $6,500 annually or $7,500 if you are 50 or older (Tretina & Schmidt, 2022).
- **Zero 401(k) borrowing**. Payroll deduction IRAs do not give employees the same financing options they often have access to through employee retirement plans.

Both regular and Roth IRAs are eligible for payroll deductions. A standard payroll deduction IRA lets you contribute pre-tax funds from your paycheck, allowing your earnings to grow tax-deferred until you collect them in retirement. Roth IRA payments are paid post-tax.

Guaranteed Income Annuities

An annuity can provide you with a consistent income throughout retirement. You can purchase an annuity with some or all of your retirement savings. An annuity offers pay either for a predetermined period of years or for life.

You can take a tax-free money transfer from your retirement plan equal to 25% of the sum used to buy an annuity. The remaining amount can be used to purchase an annuity, but your profits will be taxable. Several insurance companies provide annuities (Money Helper, n.d.).

A lifetime annuity provides a lifetime of assured income. It could be an excellent option if you want to be worry-free or are concerned about running out of money. You don't have to spend your entire pension fund on an annuity. You might purchase an annuity to cover some of your income demands rather than all of them, such as your necessities like food and housekeeping expenses. You can also buy an increasing annual annuity to hedge against inflation.

A fixed-term annuity gives you a guaranteed income for a specific time. One to forty years are your options for the term, but five to ten years are usually chosen (Money Helper, n.d.). The annuity provider invests the funds you pay for the annuity. You get paid after the period. This lump sum payment consists of the amount you contributed plus the growth of the investment. Comparing providers when considering a fixed-term annuity ensures you get the most excellent value. A variety of extra features that fit your needs can also be added.

Upgraded annuity. If you have received a medical diagnosis or have health issues that could shorten your life expectancy, a more significant retirement income may be possible for you—this annuity is also called *impaired life* (Money Helper, n.d.).

People who have held particular careers can also receive higher annuity rates from some firms. For instance, people who perform manual labor or live in areas with lower life expectancies. Before receiving an increased annuity rate offer, you will be questioned about your health.

Securities-linked annuities. You get to pick the degree of revenue that is assured to you. And to cater to this, a portion of your pension money is used. The remaining fund balance is invested, generating additional income based on investment results. In a robust economy with active investment markets, your payment would increase. However, you might only receive the minimum guaranteed amount if markets decline.

Acquired life annuity. This kind of annuity can be purchased using funds outside your pension fund. Additionally, you might buy it using the tax-free lump amount you can receive when you start drawing from your pension. Each annuity payment combines the cash invested (the capital return) and the interest component. The capital will not be subject to income tax. Only the interest portion of your annuity earnings will be taxed (Money Helper, n.d.).

What amount of annuity-derived retirement income may I expect? The following factors will determine your retirement earnings and whether you should purchase an annuity:

- How much is in your pension pot?
- What age are you when you get an annuity?
- How long you would like the annuity to last—for a particular term or a lifetime?
- Rates for annuities at the time of purchase.
- Your lifestyle and health.
- Which type of annuity, options for income, and features do you select?

Your qualification for means-tested state assistance could be affected if you take money out of your pension. If you have yet to draw benefits from your pensions, a corporation or individual you owe cash to often cannot lodge a claim against them. Before using your retirement to pay off debts, acquiring professional assistance is necessary.

When purchasing an annuity, you can pick from various options. Therefore, comparing options is crucial to determine what best suits your demands. In addition to an annuity, you have the following alternatives for spending your pension fund:

- Delay drawing from your pension and keep it where it is.
- Use your savings to generate a flexible retirement income.
- Remove a bunch of lump sum payments from your pension pot.
- Combine your options to increase your freedom.

If I Acquire an Annuity, Can I Still Contribute to My Pension?

Suppose you intend to spend a portion or all of your tax-free lump sum to considerably increase pension contributions. In that scenario, the limits on annuity recycling could apply to you. Consult a financial advisor if you are considering putting your tax-free lump sum payment back into a pension. They can aid you in determining whether returning the funds to a pension is the best course of action for you.

Retirement plans help create an additional layer to your retirement funds, frequently financially supported by employers. While only some employers offer these types of help, it is essential to ask and figure out what your options are.

Traditional IRAs are held by custodians, which include commercial banks and retail brokers. The invested funds are distributed among various investment vehicles per the instructions of the account holder and per the available options

In a Roth IRA, you can make after-tax contributions to a specific kind of tax-advantaged individual retirement account. All subsequent withdrawals from a Roth IRA are tax-free after the initial grant, which is taxed.

Payroll deduction IRAs offer a mechanism to motivate employees to save for the future. It is a simple way for workers who aren't protected by employer-sponsored retirement plans to make saving for retirement.

Contributing to an employer-sponsored retirement account is an intelligent way to save for the future. If your company doesn't offer 401(k), take advantage of Roth and traditional IRAs. We are approaching the last chapter of this book, which will discuss the fundamentals of investing.

INVESTMENT BASICS

Investing and saving are both crucial ideas for laying a solid financial foundation. The degree of risk taken is the crucial distinction between investing and saving. While saving yields a lesser return with almost no risk, investing produces a more significant return with increased risk (Royal, 2023).

While saving money is a great way to get started with your financial goals, investing it is the ultimate way to let your money work for you. This comes with potential benefits and risks that require new investors to be cautious and inform themselves before starting.

WHAT IS INVESTING?

Investing puts money to work over a long period in a project that produces profits. It involves distributing capital in the hope of making money or profit. The fundamental investment tenet anticipates favorable outcomes, whether in earnings or statistically significant price growth (Picardo, 2022).

Return and risk go hand-in-hand when investing—minimal risk typically translates into low predicted returns. In contrast, more enormous profits are usually accompanied by more risk. The returns an asset produces vary depending on the asset's nature. For instance, many equities pay quarterly dividends, whereas bonds typically pay interest every three months.

You often have to accept no risk with little or no reward when saving money. But when you invest, you risk more in the hope of greater rewards. Risk in investing is the possibility of losing some—rarely all—of the money you've put up for investment (Durana, 2022). The stock market is a prominent area to invest in whenever you're willing to take on some risk of growing your money over the long run.

Stock markets are locations where stock is traded. Here are some other investing phrases to help you.

Asset categories include stocks, bonds, real estate, and other investments with a monetary value.

Bonds are loans an investor provides for a business or government. Investors earn interest on bonds.

Diversification spreads investments across different asset categories to lower or control market volatility risks.

Funds are investment pools or baskets housing several assets.

PROS AND CONS OF INVESTING

When you take investing seriously, the income you receive from your investments can guarantee your future financial security. Your investment goals, the amount you invest, and the period you are considering will all significantly impact your expected results.

Increased investment profits. Capital gains and dividends are two ways that stock investments can produce returns. Regular payouts or coupons provided during defined periods can be obtained by investing in bonds. Real estate investments can result in capital profits and rental revenue.

Retirement strategy. While most people rely on their pay income to cover their necessities, it might be challenging to maintain a certain quality of life if one is unemployed. Many young individuals desire to retire early, meaning they must invest a considerable percentage of their income to achieve their objectives. The *FIRE* movement—financial independence, retiring early—encourages a modest lifestyle while investing and after retiring early (Dividend Earner, 2023).

Tax effectiveness. Investing in 401(k) and Roth IRAs may help save money on taxes.

Outpace inflation. Money will lose purchasing power if you don't invest it. Investing in a portfolio of assets that can outperform inflation may be a smart move to protect yourself from such a scenario.

Losses. There is never a completely risk-free investment, and you can permanently lose money. Government bonds, often considered the safest investment, are not risk free since the government may stop paying its debts (Dividend Earner, 2023).

Demands expertise. An investor with experience in several economic cycles can better handle various conditions than a beginner investment. Most people need to be trained in money; thus, they might need a financial advisor's assistance.

INVESTMENT PRINCIPLES

Many investors made questionable financial choices because they assumed they would always receive excellent returns. A wise plan contains enduring investment concepts, many of which have been overused over time. These investment principles help investors stay on pace to meet their financial goals and avoid financial mistakes.

Money is supreme. Your financial reserves will be able to support you if you leave your job or see a significant decrease in earnings.

Debt could be better. Debt-free people are usually in the best financial health. If they don't closely control their debt levels, even the most experienced investors risk getting into problems.

Knowing your timing is essential. How much risk a person can reasonably assume within their portfolio depends on how long they plan to hold it. Investing is reckless without knowing exactly when you need to spend the money.

You can generate income through portfolio rebalancing. Rebalancing changes a portfolio's weight as investment prices rise and fall to retain your original asset allocation. Selling the holdings whose value increased while increasing the assets whose value decreased is rebalancing (Shenkman, n.d.).

Diversification profits investing. A superb strategy for preventing your portfolio from becoming overly specialized in one market area is to diversify across various asset types. While employing such a technique can result in underperformers, it might guarantee that your portfolio will contain some relatively high-performing investments.

Plain over thrilling may be the best strategy. The newest trend, a special offer, or a process that claims to outperform the performance of the S&P 500 can trigger excitement. Most times, people hype these opportunities without considering their actual merit.

DIFFERENT TYPES OF INVESTMENTS

Many people find investing intimidating because there are so many possibilities, and choosing which investments are best for you can be challenging. Let's go over the most popular investing categories.

Stocks. People frequently call stocks equities or shares, arguably the most straightforward investment type. An ownership share in a publicly listed corporation is what you purchase when you buy stock. You can purchase shares in Apple, Microsoft, and many corporations (Geier, 2023).

Bonds. When you purchase a bond, you are making a loan to the issuing company. Regional governments issue municipal bonds, whereas corporations issue corporate bonds.

Mutual funds are a collection of money from several investors invested in multiple businesses. The funds may be managed actively or passively. A fund manager selects the securities to invest investors' money in an actively managed fund. Mutual funds can access various investment opportunities, including equities, bonds, and commodities.

Exchange-traded funds (ETFs) follow a market index. Investors purchase and sell ETF shares on the stock markets instead of mutual funds, which must be purchased through a fund provider (Geier, 2023). By pooling returns from all of their investments, ETFs generate revenue.

Certificates of deposit (CDs). An investment with minimal risk is called a certificate of deposit (CD). You loan a bank a specific sum in exchange for interest for a specified time. You receive your principal and the predetermined interest after that period.

Retirement programs. An investment account with specific tax advantages where participants place their funds for retirement is known as a retirement plan. Retirement plans come in various forms, including 401(k) and 403(b) schemes. Suppose your employer does not offer a retirement plan. In that case, you can open an individual retirement account (IRA) or a Roth IRA.

Options have a slightly more complicated or sophisticated technique to purchase stocks. The right to sell or buy an item at a particular price and time is purchased when you accept an option.

Annuities. When you purchase an annuity, you do it in exchange for insurance coverage that will pay you regularly. Although frequently bought years ahead, these payments typically start in retirement.

Derivatives. A financial derivative is a tool whose value is derived from another asset. It's an agreement between two parties, much like an annuity. The contract here is an arrangement to sell an item at a specific price in the future. The investor is placing a wager on the value remaining stable if they choose to buy the derivative.

Commodities. Physical goods (such as gold and crude oil) that you can invest in are commodities. Investing in things entails the possibility that prices can fluctuate owing to unforeseen circumstances. For instance, political decisions can significantly alter the price of oil. In contrast, meteorological conditions might affect the price of agricultural items.

HOW TO ASSESS YOUR INVESTMENT READINESS

Have you been debating whether to invest? The following are signs you are psychologically, intellectually, and financially prepared to trade.

You have funds for high unforeseen costs. You might have to pay for expensive dental surgery or replace your roof gutters.

You have additional funds every month. Start investing if you usually have money left over from your wage or business profits after paying your bills.

You desire increased prosperity. Consider investing in a particular business or industry that has importance for you and that you feel has value for the entire globe. If your income is regular, you may understand that investing can help you achieve your goals in life in a manner that saving your paycheck each month cannot.

Realizing you'll wish to depend on your investments rather than your income to support yourself in the future. You may consider investments such as bonds, stocks, and other types of securities to be safeguarded for your potential future.

You enjoy the thrill of living. Investing is more geared toward those aware of how intriguing and rewarding life can be when faced with risk and uncertainty (Rains, n.d.).

You are ready to learn to invest. You could gain precise lessons from your financial experiences and prevent costly blunders via financial education.

INVESTMENT STRATEGIES FOR BEGINNERS

The investing world may appear more prominent when you start alone, frequently too large. But there are several tried-and-true tactics you may use to simplify things. Here are five well-liked beginner investment techniques you may use when investing.

Buy and hold is purchasing an asset and keeping it forever. Though it's ideal never to liquidate the investment, you should aim to keep it for at least three to five years. The performance of the underlying business over time will determine your success. You must resist the urge to sell when the market is difficult if you want this technique to be successful.

Index funds involve finding a desirable stock index and purchasing an index fund based on it. The *Nasdaq Composite* and *Standard & Poor's 500* are well-known indexes (Royal, 2023). Each offers a well-diversified selection of investments by including many of the best stocks on the market.

Index plus a few occurs when an investor's portfolio combines the index fund technique and some minor investments. For example, you may dedicate 90% of your portfolio to index funds and 5% each to Amazon and Apple (if you think they have a solid long-term financial position).

Income investing amounts to owing investments that provide cash distributions, frequently dividend stocks and bonds. You receive some of your return as money, which you can spend or reinvest in further stocks and bonds. You may also benefit from capital gains if you possess income stocks.

Dollar-cost averaging involves adding money to your investments regularly. Suppose you decide to invest $500 each month. So, regardless of the state of the market, you will invest the money. Dollar-cost averaging is beneficial for establishing a consistent investing habit.

MISTAKES TO AVOID WHEN YOU START INVESTING

It's crucial to examine the best investors while studying how to invest. Still, it can also be beneficial to prepare for the worst. The top mistakes have been listed to aid investors in understanding what to look out for. It may be time to consult a financial advisor if these errors sound familiar.

Having little hope or leveraging others' expectations. Only some people can forecast or control the returns the market will offer, even after creating the ideal portfolio. Someone who does not know you, your objectives, and your current asset's location cannot determine your rate of return (Stammers, n.d.).

Not diversifying sufficiently. Some investors believe investing a significant amount of their portfolio into a single security will optimize their returns. But it might be fatal if the market shifts in the opposite direction. Excessive exposure and diversification may also negatively impact performance—strike a balance.

Buying high and selling low. Many investment choices are driven by greed or fear rather than by reason. Instead of attempting to meet long-term investment objectives, some investors buy high to maximize short-term profits.

Overspending on charges and commissions. Know the potential costs of each investing choice before creating an account. Consider investing in funds with reasonable fees and make sure the advising fees you pay are worthwhile.

Ignoring due diligence. You can look up financial management personnel in various databases to see if they have the education, working knowledge, and moral character necessary to earn your trust. Request references from them and look up their achievement on the investments they suggest.

Taking wrong risks. Too much risk-taking might result in significant differences in financial performance that may be uncomfortable for you. Achieving your financial goals may only be possible if you take too little risk.

Using the wrong consultant. In addition to having the skills to resolve your issues, the ideal financial advisor adheres to comparable investment and even life-related philosophies. The advantages of more time to discover the perfect advisor exceed the convenience of making a hasty choice (Stammers, n.d.).

Allowing emotions to interfere. Making decisions might be difficult because investing raises important emotional considerations.

- Do you want your partner to be a part of your financial planning?
- After you pass away, what do you wish to happen to your assets?

Avoid letting your emotions hinder your wealth-building investment drives.

Ignoring inflation. Remember that the things you acquire with your current assets are often more significant than their monetary value. Gain the discipline to concentrate on what matters most: your returns after accounting for rising prices.

Pursuing yield. The highest profits come with the most enormous risks, and past performance does not guarantee future results.

PITFALLS OF FOLLOWING TRENDY INVESTMENTS

Individual Stocks

Individual stock investment is when a person chooses one stock and puts all their money into it (RVV Wealth,

2021). What is your superb choice if you want to make stock market investments? Do single equities in your portfolio make sense, or should you choose ETFs or mutual funds instead?

While there are numerous things to consider in this situation, another investment idea also comes into play. Modern portfolio theory seeks to balance risk reduction with return maximization. A mutual fund or ETF is likely a better choice if you lack the finances to make this happen (Travillian, 2022).

Pros

- Buying individual stocks results in lower fees. The annual management charge you previously paid to the fund company for managing your investments is no longer due. Instead, a fee is charged when you buy and sell shares.
- Managing the taxes on your personal stocks is simpler.

Cons

- Diversification is challenging to achieve.
- You need more time to examine your portfolio since you must ensure that the businesses

you've put your money into are not experiencing problems.

Since individual stocks make diversification challenging or unattainable, it could be a better investing strategy (RVV Wealth, 2021).

Crypto

Millions of new investors venture into the volatile and unregulated cryptocurrency industry every year. But regrettably, many people choose their assets poorly and inadvertently (Finance Monthly, 2022). These tips will help you succeed with your cryptocurrency investing.

Proper research. Cross-reference essential information from several trustworthy sources to ensure you receive the best service.

Avoid single crypto trading. Losses are minimized by diversifying a portfolio over several crypto-assets, such as Ether, DeFi, and stablecoins. Price correlation is the most important thing to consider when spreading your Bitcoin holdings. You should make as much effort as possible to hold lag-free digital materials.

Prioritize security. Data loss or theft and the possibility of someone learning what you purchased are all risks associated with local storage. The safe deposit box where users keep their bitcoins must separate each user's public and private keys.

Be cautious. Triple checking is required for every cryptographic transaction. If you're a novice investor, seek expert advice before investing in crypto.

Non-Fungible Tokens (NFTs)

Although NFTs are receiving a lot of focus, this new territory is ripe for fraud and expensive blunders for many people. Both investors and creators must take precautions against everything from clicking on a phony link to trying to day trade their way to riches using NFTs. Avoid these common blunders if you're trying to invest.

Cheap NFTs. NFTs are being produced by everyone, some of which may be brand-new, inexpensive, or even serve as a cover for illegal activity. Research the project online, on Twitter, and on the Discord channel before you purchase an NFT.

Day-trading deals. NFTs are vulnerable to astronomical price swings. These variations may persuade you that an NFT is an excellent investment to buy, keep for a few weeks, and then sell for a profit (Maganis, n.d.). This is occasionally true, but it carries a significant risk and is best left to knowledgeable NFT investors. Instead, concentrate on NFTs from artists you respect.

Illiquid NFTs. Invest in a collection with a low rate of return. You can find that no investors are still interested in the project even after the price reduces. This is why you ought to invest in value-based NFT ventures rather than falling for their marketing gimmick.

Scams. Purchasing your NFTs through shady links is one of the worst blunders you could make. These con artists send out phony links that draw unwary investors and empty their wallets by exploiting the hype surrounding an NFT collection. Use only the URLs on the project team's social media and official website.

INVESTING WITH MUTUAL FUNDS

A mutual fund pools shareholder money to buy different assets, including equities and bonds. Experienced money managers oversee mutual funds and distribute the assets to boost investors' income or capital gains (Hayes, 2023).

The efficiency of the securities that the mutual fund invests in determines the fund's value. Investors purchase the performance of a mutual fund's portfolio when they purchase a unit or share of the fund. The fund receives revenue from stock dividends and interest on bonds held in its portfolio. It distributes nearly all of this income to fund owners each year.

Fund investors can frequently receive a cheque for dividends or reinvest the earnings to buy more mutual fund shares. When a fund sells an investment with appreciated value, it gains capital, which most funds distribute to investors.

Mutual fund varieties are:

- **Stock funds** primarily invest in equities or stocks.
- **Bond funds** are frequently actively managed to purchase relatively discounted bonds to resell them for a profit.
- **Index funds** invest in equities that track a significant market index like the S&P 500 (Hayes, 2023).
- **Balanced funds**. Bonds, money market instruments, and stocks are all included in the mix of asset classes that balanced funds invest in.
- **Income funds** offer consistent income by investing in reputable corporate and government bonds, holding them until maturity.

Exchange-traded funds (ETFs) have the advantages of stocks and being set up as investment trusts that trade on stock markets. You can purchase and sell ETFs at any time throughout the transaction day. ETFs often charge less in fees than mutual funds. Mutual funds are usually more affordable and liquid.

Mutual Fund Fees

A mutual fund may charge shareholders annual running costs. The expense ratio, typically from 1% to 3% of the funds under administration, represents the yearly proportion of annual fund operating fees. An investment fund's expense ratio is calculated by adding its advisory or management charge and operating expenses (Hayes, 2023).

Shareholder fees are the commissions, sales, and redemption costs investors pay when buying or selling mutual funds. Some funds impose additional charges and fines for withdrawing funds early or selling a holding before a predetermined period has passed.

Most individual investors currently use a broker to buy mutual funds with A-shares. Financial advisors who provide these products might persuade customers to purchase higher-load options to earn commissions. Class B shares are those funds that impose management and other fees upon the sale of an investor's ownership.

Pros

- Diversification can be attained more quickly and affordably by investing in a mutual fund rather than buying individual stocks.
- Mutual funds are highly liquid investments since they trade on the major stock markets and may be purchased and sold quickly.
- A mutual fund's transaction expenses are lower than what a person would spend on securities transactions since it purchases and sells large quantities of securities at once.

Cons

- Your mutual fund's value could decrease anytime without an assurance of return.
- To satisfy daily share redemptions, mutual funds must hold a sizeable portion of their holdings in cash.
- Mutual funds offer expert management to investors, but fees lower the fund's ultimate payout. They are charged to investors irrespective of the fund's success.

Instead of purchasing mutual fund shares from other investors, purchase them directly from the fund or via a broker for the fund. Thoroughly study the prospectus before investing in mutual fund shares. Information about the investment goals, risks, performance, and costs of the mutual fund is included in the prospectus (Investor.gov, n.d.).

SHOULD YOU USE A FINANCIAL ADVISOR?

You have the option of conducting your own research. Still, to do it well, you'll need to invest a lot of time staying current on all the developments across various topics. For example, legislation governing investing and insurance change. Tax rules and other laws may also change, affecting your financial situation.

Changes to the mutual fund selection at your brokerage business may significantly affect your financial status. You must choose where to deposit the money if one of your funds collapses. You'll also need to keep up with the release of new financial solutions if you wish to manage your finances independently. A financial counselor or advisor can help with all these, which lowers your cognitive load and considerably streamlines the investing process.

You might need the services of a fiduciary—a fiduciary is a person or business required to uphold the highest moral principles and prioritize clients' interests (Hube, 2022). Fiduciaries operate in the best interests of their clients and deliver timely, accurate reports. They also charge fair prices, promptly fulfill orders, and declare any conflicts of interest. The annual fee for fiduciaries is typically a proportion of the assets. Customers with simple needs could be happy with commission-based services and spend less over time. These are the categories of financial advisors you might consider hiring:

Robo advisors are online financial services. You won't meet with an advisor in person when using Robo advisors. Computer algorithms provide feedback and answer your queries once you input your data (Jones, n.d.).

Online financial planners offer comparable services to robo-advisors but give you access to a qualified advisor. Remember that the advisor could occasionally change, making it challenging to establish a connection and find someone who genuinely gets you and your objectives.

Traditional financial counselors. Your devoted financial advisor should spend time getting to know you and learning about the people and things that are most important to you.

Choosing a licensed financial planner is one of your most significant financial choices. To find a fantastic one, follow these steps.

Analyze your needs. Look for someone with experience adjusting budgets and counseling clients to live within their means when dealing with debt or increasing retirement savings.

Choose planners who meet your goals. You can rely on a CFP (certified financial planner) to have received in-depth training, aced a demanding exam, and be qualified to give you advice on a variety of financial topics.

Review the costs. Focus your search on fee-only advisers that don't collect commissions for recommending financial products to you but charge for asset management and guidance. Some impose hourly rates, which can be between $100 and $400 (Braverman, 2022).

Examine the candidates. Set an appointment to speak with the top two or three applicants, ideally in person. A lot of reputable financial advisors provide a no-cost initial consultation. Verify their background working with clients in comparable situations. Inquire about how they handled a circumstance similar to yours.

USING YOUR INVESTMENTS TO GET YOU EVEN MORE MONEY

Suppose you want to spend $500,000 on significant renovations to your house. After asking your bank for a regular loan for the entire amount, you are offered a 5% APR (the annual percentage rate). But because you own a portfolio of blue-chip stocks worth $1,000,000, you use those assets as collateral for the loan and get an improved APR of 3.25%.

Your lender offers a lower interest rate because they view the pledged securities as an additional layer of safety. You appreciate financial aid since it enables you to retain your stock investments and borrow money at a lesser rate. This is how security-based lending (SBL) works.

Security-based lending is the process of acquiring loans using securities as collateral. It offers quick access to funds for investing in a business and real estate (Downey, 2020). SBL, which large financial institutions and private banks typically provide, is available to persons with significant capital and wealth. People may take securities based loans to complete substantial deals to make a vital business acquisition.

SBL vs. securities lending. Unlike SBL, which uses securities as a deposit for a loan, securities lending needs collateral in a letter of credit (or in cash). Usually, individual investors are excluded from securities lending. Instead, it happens between dealers and/or investment brokers who sign an agreement that describes the type of loan—the conditions, duration, fees, and collateral.

Pros

- SBL eliminates the requirement to sell securities, preventing a taxable event for the investor and guaranteeing the continuance of the investor's investment plan.
- It provides access to cash in a matter of days at reduced interest rates with much repayment flexibility.
- It offers a second, attractive source of income with little added risk.

Cons

- Financial analysts are growing more apprehensive as interest rates rise that there would be forced liquidations and fire sales if the market flips.
- Although financial regulators alert investors to the hazards associated with this market, no organization monitors securities lending.

Ryan Cutter invested significantly in *Kinder Morgan*, an energy infrastructure provider, but lost nearly a third of his money. Instead of giving up, he learned what to look for in an organization's balance statement. He gave essential metrics like the price-to-earnings ratios more consideration.

Cutter purchased more stock during the market crash last year. His *Chevron* (CVX) and *Disney* (DIS) investments yielded significant profits. He diversified by moving a portion of his portfolio offshore. These victories offset his losses from Kinder Morgan. Cutter's portfolio finishes the year's considerable gain.

    Investing and saving are both crucial ideas for laying a solid financial foundation. The degree of risk taken is the main distinction between investing and saving. While saving yields a lesser return with almost no risk, investing produces a more significant return with increased risk.

    Investing puts money to work over a long period in a project that produces profits. It involves distributing capital in the hope of making money or profit. The fundamental investment tenet anticipates favorable outcomes, whether in earnings or statistically significant price growth.

    Many people find investing intimidating because there are so many possibilities, and choosing which investments are best for you can be challenging.

    It's crucial to examine the best investors while studying how to invest. Still, it can also be beneficial to prepare for the worst.

    You might need the services of a fiduciary—a fiduciary is a person or business required to uphold the highest moral principles and prioritize clients' interests. Fiduciaries operate in the best interests of their clients and deliver timely, accurate reports.

Idle cash doesn't grow; nobody becomes a millionaire by just keeping their money in the bank. If you want to create wealth, embrace investing—make money grow itself! We have reached the end of this book, but you can read the upcoming conclusion for a refresher on everything you've learned.`

CONCLUSION

This book sets you up for the financial future of your dreams. It guides you into adulthood with the knowledge you need to build wealth and master your finances. It provides timeless advice on the most critical factors of money management, budgeting, investing, and more so that young professionals can quickly build healthy financial habits and know how to achieve their monetary goals.

Use the information to start your money management and budgeting efforts immediately. Many young adults feel overwhelmed and frustrated at the beginning of this process. Still, it gets easier and even more enjoyable over time.

These are the key takeaways from this book:

- Core aspects of financial literacy and creative strategies to successfully build wealth.
- Innovative strategies for establishing realistic yet challenging goals, achieving them, avoiding financial mistakes, and preparing for retirement.
- Practical ways to understand bank interest rates and create the account type that supports short or long-term financial objectives.
- Clever tips for eliminating unhealthy choices, making people splurge, boosting savings capacity, bypassing the common pitfalls threatening budgets, and building credit rating.
- Helpful methods for discovering basic loan types, including their characteristics, learning practical procedures for comparing loan conditions when requiring credits, and understanding effortless debt repayment.
- Efficient wealth-building investment vehicles and strategies plus successful tips.

Remember Ryan Cutter—he didn't give up after losing nearly a quarter of his *Kinder Morgan* asset. His subsequent investments in *Chevron* and *Disney* offset the previous setback. If your investment does not perform as you want, discover and fix the problem. You have the essential tools in this book; use them.

Your financial future is in your hands—the faster you start acting on it, the more you'll be able to achieve!

Kindly hit us with a review if you enjoyed this book.

REFERENCES

Abraham, S. (2018, August 14). *5 mistakes you should avoid when setting financial goals.* Retrieved March 26, 2023, from https://www.livemint.com/Money/iQCo6jSxDncC6zkPIs39LL/5-mistakes-you-should-avoid-when-setting-financial-goals.html

Akin, J. (2019, October 3). *What Is Credit?* Retrieved April 1, 2023, from https://www.experian.com/blogs/ask-experian/credit-education/faqs/what-is-credit/

Appleby, D. (2023, April 4). *Participate in an Employer-Sponsored Retirement Plan.* Retrieved April 9, 2023, from https://www.investopedia.com/retirement/reasons-use-employer-sponsored-retirement-plan/

Axelton, K. (2021, October 13). *8 Different Types of Loans You Should Know.* Retrieved April 4, 2023, from https://www.experian.com/blogs/ask-experian/types-of-loans/

Banton, C. (2023, March 28). *Interest Rates: Different Types and What They Mean to Borrowers.* Retrieved April 4, 2023, from https://www.investopedia.com/terms/i/interestrate.asp

Bareham, H. (2022, October 19). *How to redeem credit card rewards.* Retrieved April 1, 2023, from https://www.bankrate.com/finance/credit-cards/how-to-redeem-credit-card-rewards/

Bell, A. (2022, April 7). *What Are the 5 Purposes of Budgeting?* Retrieved March 28, 2023, from https://www.investopedia.com/financial-edge/1109/6-reasons-why-you-need-a-budget.aspx

Bitpanda. (n.d.). *What is personal finance and why does it matter?* Retrieved March 23, 2023, from https://www.bitpanda.com/academy/en/lessons/what-is-personal-finance-and-why-does-it-matter/

BOA. (n.d.). *Creating a budget.* Retrieved March 30, 2023, from https://bettermoneyhabits.bankofamerica.com/en/saving-budgeting/creating-a-budget

Braverman, B. (2022, October 6). How to Find a Good Financial

Planner. Retrieved April 12, 2023, from https://www.consumerreports.org/money/financial-planning/how-to-find-a-good-financial-planner-a5822372703/

BTG. (n.d.). *How Often Should You Review Your Budget?* Retrieved March 30, 2023, from https://bethebudget.com/how-often-should-you-review-your-budget/

Campbell, J. (2018, April 12). *How to Compare Loan Terms.* Retrieved April 4, 2023, from https://www.moneymanagement.org/blog/how-to-compare-loan-terms

Capital One. (2021, July 29). *Types of Debt.* Retrieved April 5, 2023, from https://www.capitalone.com/learn-grow/money-management/types-of-debt/

Carlson, R. (2022, September 13). *How to Calculate Your Interest Rate for a Bank Loan.* Retrieved April 4, 2023, from https://www.thebalancemoney.com/how-to-calculate-interest-rates-393165

CCS. (n.d.). *Manage Money Better.* Retrieved March 26, 2023, from https://nomoredebts.org/blog/manage-money-better/financial-goals-feel-unrealistic

Central Bank. (n.d.). *10 Strategies to Avoid Getting into Debt.* Retrieved April 8, 2023, from https://www.centralbank.net/learning-center/strategies-to-avoid-debt/

CFI. (2022, December 18). *Employee Stock Ownership Plan (ESOP).* Retrieved April 10, 2023, from https://corporatefinanceinstitute.com/resources/career/employee-stock-ownership-plan-esop/

CFI. (2023, January 8). *Lender.* Retrieved April 4, 2023, from https://corporatefinanceinstitute.com/resources/commercial-lending/lender/#:~:text=A%20lender%20is%20a%20financial,the%20total%20amount%20of%20loan.

CFI. (2023, January 8). *Debt.* Retrieved April 5, 2023, from https://corporatefinanceinstitute.com/resources/commercial-lending/debt/

CFI. (2023, March 19). *Money Management.* Retrieved March 23, 2023, from https://corporatefinanceinstitute.com/resources/capital-markets/money-management/

CFPB. (n.d.). *An essential guide to building an emergency fund.* Retrieved

REFERENCES | 201

March 30, 2023, from https://www.consumerfinance.gov/an-essential-guide-to-building-an-emergency-fund/

Chen, J. (2022, May 25). *Money Management: Definition and Top Money Managers by Assets.* Retrieved March 23, 2023, from https://www.investopedia.com/terms/m/moneymanagement.asp

Chen, J. (2023, February 28). *Debt: What It Is, How It Works, Types, and Ways to Pay Back.* Retrieved April 5, 2023, from https://www.investopedia.com/terms/d/debt.asp

CNN Money. (n.d.). *Ultimate guide to retirement.* Retrieved April 9, 2023, from https://money.cnn.com/retirement/guide/basics_basics.moneymag/index.htm

Connect. (2018, August 14). *Personal loans vs mortgage loans: best for buying a home?* Retrieved April 4, 2023, from https://cannect.ca/personal-loans-vs-mortgage-loans/

Cruze, R. (2022, December 22). *How to Set Financial Goals.* Retrieved March 26, 2023, from https://www.ramseysolutions.com/personal-growth/setting-financial-goals

Debt.org (n.d.). *Credit.* Retrieved April 1, 2023, from https://www.debt.org/credit/

DeNicola, L. (2020, May 24). *Your guide to bank accounts in the United States.* Retrieved March 24, 2023, from https://www.novacredit.com/resources/a-guide-to-the-different-types-of-bank-accounts-in-the-united-states

Dividend Earner. (2023, January 4). *Top 5 Reasons Why Investing Is Important.* Retrieved April 12, 2023, from https://dividendearner.com/why-investing-is-important/

Downey, L. (2020, August 26). Securities-Based Lending: Advantages, Risks and Examples. Retrieved April 12, 2023, from https://www.investopedia.com/terms/s/securitiesbased-lending.asp

Durana, A. (2022, December 12). *What Is Investing?* Retrieved April 12, 2023, from https://www.nerdwallet.com/article/investing/what-is-investing

Equifax. (n.d.). *What Is a Credit Score?* Retrieved April 1, 2023, from https://www.equifax.com/personal/education/credit/score/what-is-a-credit-score/

REFERENCES

Equifax. (n.d.). *How to Improve Your Credit Score*. Retrieved April 1, 2023, from https://www.equifax.com/personal/education/credit/score/how-to-improve-credit-score/

Finance Monthly. (2022, November 28). Top 5 Mistakes Every Crypto Investor Must Avoid. Retrieved April 12, 2023, from https://www.finance-monthly.com/2022/11/top-5-mistakes-every-crypto-investor-must-avoid/

Financial Bank. (n.d.). *10 Common Budgeting Mistakes (and How to Fix Them)*. Retrieved March 28, 2023, from https://students.1fbusa.com/money-smarts/common-budgeting-mistakes-and-how-to-fix-them

FindLaw. (2023, January 09). *Types of Lenders*. Retrieved April 4, 2023, from https://www.findlaw.com/realestate/mortgages-equity-loans/types-of-lenders.html

FNBO. (2021, November 8). *Do I Really Need a Checking Account? Yes, and Here's Why*. Retrieved March 24, 2023, from https://www.fnbo.com/insights/2021/personal-finance/do-i-need-checking-account/#:~:text=Your%20checking%20account%20can%20act,making%20purchases%2C%20and%20paying%20bills.

Fontinelle, A. (2022, October 8). *How to Set Financial Goals for Your Future*. Retrieved March 26, 2023, from https://www.investopedia.com/articles/personal-finance/100516/setting-financial-goals/

Fresh Books. (2023, February 27). *SEP IRA Plan: What is Simplified Employee Pension Plan?* Retrieved April 10, 2023, from https://www.freshbooks.com/glossary/tax/sep-ira-plan?psafe_param=1&ref=&campaignid=16988866217&adgroupid=&targetid=&crid=&dv=c&geo=9000681&ntwk=x&source=GOOGLE&qgad=&qgterm=&gclid=CjwKCAiAr4GgBhBFEiwAgwORrfrk_dNjdb5VVDpzEYl7bN33J_N5gslE8dc2nSpQ1hq2OUnRZVLHKRoCcD0QAvD_BwE

Fullerton Markets. (2021, January 20). *How to Effectively Set SMART Financial Goals and Actually Achieve Them*. Retrieved March 26, 2023, from https://www.fullertonmarkets.com/blog/how-to-effectively-set-smart-financial-goals-and-actually-achieve-them

Ganti, A. (2022, May 27). *What Is a Budget? Plus 10 Budgeting Myths*

Holding You Back. Retrieved March 28, 2023, from https://www.investopedia.com/terms/b/budget.asp

Geier, B. (2023, March 17). *10 Common Types of Investments and How They Work.* Retrieved April 12, 2023, from https://smartasset.com/investing/types-of-investment

George, D. (2023, February 13). *What Is a Good Interest Rate for a Personal Loan?* Retrieved April 4, 2023, from https://www.fool.com/the-ascent/personal-loans/what-is-good-interest-rate-personal-loan/

Gillespie, L. (2023, January 13). *Average American debt statistics.* Retrieved April 4, 2023, from https://www.bankrate.com/personal-finance/debt/average-american-debt/

Gogol, F. (2022, November 4). *Principal Vs. Interest: What's the Difference?* Retrieved April 4, 2023, from https://www.stilt.com/blog/2018/11/principal-vs-interest/

Gravier, E. (2022, December 29). *The 5 types of expenses experts say you should never charge on a credit card.* Retrieved April 1, 2023, from https://www.cnbc.com/select/expenses-never-put-on-credit-card/

Great Lakes. (n.d.). *Budgeting & Money Management for Students.* Retrieved March 28, 2023, from https://mygreatlakes.org/educate/knowledge-center/successful-budgeting.html#:~:text=But%20what%20exactly%20is%20budgeting,keep%20their%20finances%20in%20order.

Hagen, K. (2023, February 6). *403(b) Retirement Plans for Teachers & Non-Profit Employees.* Retrieved April 10, 2023, from https://www.fool.com/retirement/plans/403b/

Haughn, R. (2023, February 2). *The top 9 reasons for personal loans.* Retrieved April 4, 2023, from https://www.bankrate.com/loans/personal-loans/top-reasons-to-apply-for-personal-loan/

Hayes, A. (2023, February 21). *Understanding a Traditional IRA vs. Other Retirement Accounts.* Retrieved April 10, 2023, from https://www.investopedia.com/terms/t/traditionalira.asp

Hayes, A. (2023, March 13). Mutual Funds: Different Types and How They Are Priced. Retrieved April 12, 2023, from https://www.investopedia.com/terms/m/mutualfund.asp

REFERENCES

Hoffman, M. (2023, March 29). *What is a credit card?* Retrieved April 1, 2023, from https://www.bankrate.com/finance/credit-cards/what-is-a-credit-card/

Horymski, C. (2023, February 24). *Average Consumer Debt Levels Increase in 2022.* Retrieved April 5, 2023, from https://www.experian.com/blogs/ask-experian/research/consumer-debt-study/

Hube, K. (2022, May 12). What Is a Fiduciary, and Do I Need One? Retrieved April 12, 2023, from https://www.barrons.com/advisor/articles/what-is-a-fiduciary-and-do-i-need-one-51652382854

Investor.gov (n.d.). Mutual funds. Retrieved April 12, 2023, from https://www.investor.gov/introduction-investing/investing-basics/investment-products/mutual-funds-and-exchange-traded-1

Jones, E. (n.d.). *What is a 457 plan?* Retrieved April 10, 2023, from https://www.edwardjones.com/us-en/investment-services/account-options/retirement/457-plans

Jones, E. (n.d.). How to choose a financial advisor. Retrieved April 12, 2023, from https://www.edwardjones.ca/ca-en/working-financial-advisor/how-choose-financial-advisor?utm_source=google&utm_medium=cpc&utm_campaign=dsa-17095410446-134019204417-dsa-1536418750204&gclid=CjwKCAiAr4GgBhBFEiwAgwORrYVe-XwgeenPHanat6-2iDkO6W7rPAxtuzZs20pjFArcHuxvoX_3pxoCZXgQAvD_BwE

Kagan, J. (2021, April 19). *What Is a Loan, How Does It Work, Types, and Tips on Getting One.* Retrieved April 4, 2023, from https://www.investopedia.com/terms/l/loan.asp

Karl, S. (2021, November 3). *What Is a High-Yield Savings Account?* Retrieved March 24, 2023, from https://www.investopedia.com/articles/pf/09/high-yield-savings-account.asp

Kopp, C. (2021, November 3). *How Interest Works on Savings Accounts.* Retrieved March 24, 2023, from https://www.investopedia.com/articles/personal-finance/062315/how-interest-rates-work-savings-accounts.asp

Lambarena, M. & Tierney, S. (2021, November 24). *How to Choose a Bank.* Retrieved March 24, 2023, from https://www.nerdwallet.com/article/banking/how-to-choose-a-bank

REFERENCES | 205

Latimer, G. (n.d.). *Benefits of a Bank Account.* Retrieved March 24, 2023, from https://consumer.westchestergov.com/financial-education/money-management/benefits-of-a-bank-account

Lockert, M. (2022, October 21). *What is a budget?* Retrieved March 28, 2023, from https://fortune.com/recommends/banking/what-is-a-budget/

Maganis, J. (n.d.). Top NFTs Mistakes to Avoid. Retrieved April 12, 2023, from https://crowdcreate.us/top-nfts-mistakes-to-avoid/

Money Gate. (2023, January 23). *New trends in banking 2023.* Retrieved March 24, 2023, from https://money-gate.com/new-trends-in-banking-2023/

Money Helper. (n.d.). *Beginner's guide to managing your money.* Retrieved March 23, 2023, from https://www.moneyhelper.org.uk/en/everyday-money/budgeting/beginners-guide-to-managing-your-money

Money Helper. (n.d.). *Guaranteed retirement income (annuities) explained.* Retrieved April 10, 2023, from https://www.moneyhelper.org.uk/en/pensions-and-retirement/taking-your-pension/guaranteed-retirement-income-annuities-explained

Money Lover. (n.d.). *What is Money Management? Definition & Example.* Retrieved March 23, 2023, from https://note.moneylover.me/money-management/

Money Nuggets. (n.d.). *7 Reasons You Need to Set Financial Goals.* Retrieved March 26, 2023, from https://www.moneynuggets.co.uk/important-to-set-financial-goals/

Muller, C. (2023, March 27). *How Much of Your Paycheck Should You Save? Budgeting Basics for Gen Z.* Retrieves March 30, 2023, from https://www.moneyunder30.com/percentage-of-income-should-you-save-every-month

Opperman, M. (n.d.). *10 Basic Rules of Money Management.* Retrieved March 23, 2023, from https://credit.org/blog/10-basic-rules-of-money-management/

O'Shea, B. & Barroso, A. (2022, October 27). *5 Tips for Lowering Your Credit Utilization.* Retrieved April 1, 2023, from https://www.nerdwallet.com/article/finance/tips-for-lowering-credit-utilization#:~:text=Make%20a%20habit%20of%20patrolling,switch%20to%20us ing%20another%20card.&text=Simply%20getting%20into%20the%20habit,you%20decrease%20your%20credit%20usage.

O'Shea, B. & Schwahn, L. (2022, December 2). *Budgeting 101: How to Budget Money.* Retrieved March 30, 2023, from https://www.nerdwallet.com/article/finance/how-to-budget

Pant, P. (n.d.). *How much should I save each month?* Retrieved March 30, 2023, from https://www.tiaa.org/public/learn/personal-finance-101/how-much-of-my-income-should-i-save-every-month

Paris, D. (2023, January 6). *8 Reasons Why Financial Literacy Is Important.* Retrieved March 23, 2023, from https://www.mydoh.ca/learn/money-101/money-basics/8-reasons-to-teach-financial-literacy-to-kids-teens/

Paul, T. (2022, July 8). *Is 800 a good credit score? Here's what to expect when you reach this number.* Retrieved March 31, 2023, from https://www.google.com/amp/s/www.cnbc.com/amp/select/is-800-a-good-credit-score-heres-what-it-means/

Paychex. (2023, January 5). *The Pooled Employer 401(k) Plan (PEP): 5 Big Benefits for Your Small Business.* Retrieved April 9, 2023, from https://www.paychex.com/articles/employee-benefits/pooled-employer-plan#:~:text=for%20large%20companies.-,What%20is%20a%20Pooled%20Employer%20401(k)%20Plan%3F,such%20as%20a%20trade%20group).

Phipps, M. (2022, May 31). *What Is a Profit-Sharing Plan?* Retrieved April 10, 2023, from https://www.thebalancemoney.com/profit-sharing-plan-2894303

Piburn, J. (2022, January 31). *What is 401(k) matching and how does it work?* Retrieved April 9, 2023, from https://www.empower.com/the-currency/work/how-does-401k-matching-work#:~:text=A%20partial%20match%20means%20that,to%206%25%20of%20your%20salary.

Picardo, E. (2022, July 22). *Investing Explained: Types of Investments and How To Get Started.* Retrieved April 12, 2023, from https://www.investopedia.com/terms/i/investing.asp

Rains, J. (n.d.). *7 Signs You're Ready to Invest.* Retrieved April 12, 2023, from https://investingtothrive.com/7-signs-you-are-ready-to-invest/

Ramsey Solutions. (2022, December 9). *4 Most Common Types of Bank Accounts*. Retrieved March 24, 2023, from https://www.ramseysolutions.com/banking/types-of-bank-accounts

Ramsey Solutions. (2023, January 11). *What Do You Need to Know About Financial Literacy?* Retrieved March 23, 2023, from https://www.ramseysolutions.com/financial-literacy/what-is-financial-literacy

Ritchie, A. (2023, March 20). *Financial Literacy*. Retrieved March 23, 2023, from https://www.annuity.org/financial-literacy/

Royal, J. (2023, January 24). 5 popular investment strategies for beginners. Retrieved April 12, 2023, from https://www.bankrate.com/investing/investment-strategies-for-beginners/

Royal, J. (2023, January 25). *Saving vs. investing: How are they different and which is better?* Retrieved April 12, 2023, from https://www.bankrate.com/investing/saving-vs-investing/#:~:text=The%20biggest%20difference%20between%20saving,in%20order%20to%20do%20so.

RVV Wealth. (2021, September 1). Why Individual Stock Selection Is A Bad Approach To Investing. Retrieved April 12, 2023, from https://rvwwealth.com/why-individual-stock-selection-is-a-bad-approach-to-investing/

Schwahn, L. (2020, December 18). *What Is a Budget?* Retrieved March 28, 2023, from https://www.nerdwallet.com/article/finance/what-is-a-budget

Segal, T. (2023, March 31). *Roth IRA: What It Is and How to Open One*. Retrieved April 10, 2023, from https://www.investopedia.com/terms/r/rothira.asp

Shenkman, J. (n.d.). *10 timeless investing principles*. Retrieved April 12, 2023, from https://www.fidelity.ca/en/investor/investorinsights/timelessinvestingprinciples/

Stammers, R. (n.d.). Tips for Avoiding the Top 20 Common Investment Mistakes. Retrieved April 12, 2023, from https://www.cfainstitute.org/-/media/documents/support/future-finance/avoiding-commoninvestor-mistakes.pdf

Stinnett, J. (2023, March 13). *How Nonqualified Deferred Compensation (NQDC) Plans Work*. Retrieved April 10, 2023, from https://smartasset.com/retirement/how-do-non-qualified-deferred-compensation-plans-work

Tarpley, L. (2022, April 5). *8 tips for choosing the best bank*. Retrieved March 24, 2023, from https://www.businessinsider.com/personal-finance/how-to-choose-a-bank?r=US&IR=T

The Hartford. (n.d.). *What Is a SIMPLE IRA and How Does It Work?* Retrieved April 10, 2023, from https://www.thehartford.com/business-insurance/strategy/small-business-retirement-plans/simple-ira

Travillian, A. (2022, January 26). Single Stocks in Your Portfolio: Pros and Con. Retrieved April 12, 2023, from https://www.investopedia.com/articles/investing/072915/single-stocks-your-portfolio-pros-and-cons.asp

Tretina, K. & Schmidt, J. (2022, October 24). *What Is A Payroll Deduction IRA?* Retrieved April 10, 2023, from https://www.forbes.com/advisor/retirement/payroll-deduction-ira/

USAGCR. (n.d.). *Credit Reports and Scores*. Retrieved April 1, 2023, from https://www.usa.gov/credit-reports

USDL. (2011, November 1). *Fact Sheet: Cash Balance Pension Plans*. Retrieved April 10, 2023, from https://www.dol.gov/agencies/ebsa/about-ebsa/our-activities/resource-center/fact-sheets/cash-balance-pension-plans

Waugh, E. (2022, April 11). *How to Set SMART Financial Goals*. Retrieved March 26, 2023, from https://www.experian.com/blogs/ask-experian/how-to-set-smart-financial-goals/

Wells Fargo. (n.d.). *Adjusting your financial plan*. Retrieved March 26, 2023, from https://www.wellsfargo.com/financial-education/basic-finances/build-the-future/short-long-term-planning/financial-plan-adjustments/

Wells Fargo. (n.d.). *How your credit score is calculated*. Retrieved April 1, 2023, from https://www.wellsfargo.com/financial-education/credit-management/calculate-credit-score/

Westchester County. (n.d.). *Tips to Reduce Your Debt*. Retrieved April 8,

2023, from https://consumer.westchestergov.com/financial-education/credit-and-debt-management/tips-to-reduce-your-debt

WFP. (n.d.). *Why You Should Regularly Review Your Financial Plans.* Retrieved March 26, 2023, from https://woodruff-fp.co.uk/why-you-should-regularly-review-your-financial-plans/

White, A. (2023, March 30). *What happens when you miss a credit card payment?* Retrieved April 1, 2023, from https://www.cnbc.com/select/what-happens-when-you-miss-a-credit-card-payment/

White, J. (2022, May 15). *How Long Does It Take to Get a Credit Score After Opening an Account?* Retrieved April 1, 2023, from https://www.experian.com/blogs/ask-experian/how-long-after-getting-first-credit-account-will-score-created/

WSM. (n.d.). *Borrower.* Retrieved April 4, 2023, from https://www.wallstreetmojo.com/borrower/

Yochim, D. (2023, February 23). *What Is a 401(k) Plan?* Retrieved April 9, 2023, from https://www.nerdwallet.com/article/investing/what-is-a-401k

Made in United States
Orlando, FL
10 December 2024